Jeanne Jugan

This book belongs to:
Fran E. Murphy
215-482-6284

JEANNE JUGAN

Humble, so as to love more

PAUL MILCENT

Translated by
Alan Neame

DARTON · LONGMAN + TODD

First published in Great Britain in 1980
Darton, Longman and Todd Ltd
1 Spencer Court
140–142 Wandsworth High Street
London SW18 4JJ

Second edition 2000

Originally published in French as *Jeanne Jugan: Humble Pour Aimer*,
Les Editions du Centurion, Paris, 1978. Reprinted 1996, Bayard
Éditions/Centurion. Translated into English, Spanish, Italian,
Portuguese, Dutch, Arabic, Chinese, Korean, Marathi and Telugu.

ISBN 0–232–52383–5

NIHIL OBSTAT: Rome, 24 July 1979, A. P. Frutaz,
Under-Secretary of the Congregation for the Causes of Saints;
Westminster, R. J. Cumming, DD, Censor.

IMPRIMATUR: Mgr David Norris, VG,
Westminster, 5 November, 1979.

Printed in Great Britain by
Page Bros, Norwich, Norfolk

CONTENTS

PREFACE

This book appears under a single author's name.

But this is hardly just, since the book is in fact the product of close co-operation. For in the Archives of the Little Sisters of the Poor, not only did I find extensive documentation of the life of Jeanne Jugan—the result of immensely patient, methodical, critical and wholly admirable hard work—but I was also given extremely useful guidance and excellent advice. The research had already been done; all that was left for me to do was to steep myself in it, verify the quality of the work, and absorb the contents of those documents, spending almost a year in Jeanne Jugan's company as it were, and then give expression to the idea I had conceived of her and her existence. This really deserves better than passing acknowledgment.

Furthermore, I constantly referred to the text of the *Positio super Virtutibus*, to check my own conclusions against those of this important work, which has led to the official recognition of the heroism of Jeanne Jugan's virtues by Jean-Paul II on 13 July 1979.

Other people have helped me too by kindly reading and commenting on my manuscript. I thank them most sincerely.

PM

The Author

Paul Milcent was born in Normandy in 1923 and became a priest in the Eudist Congregation (a society of priests) in 1949. He spent some time as a professor in a college, then was in formation work in the Congregation, before becoming an adviser to religious communities. He is very much interested in the spiritual tradition of Bérulle and St John Eudes, especially the help it can bring to the Apostolate today.

INTRODUCTION

Forty-seven years of fairly commonplace existence. Twelve years of intense evangelical creativity. Twenty-seven years of silent and hidden inactivity. As the summary of a long life, this is an unusual one, and the reasons for the protracted retirement are even more disconcerting. But such was the life of Jeanne Jugan, foundress of the Little Sisters of the Poor, from 1792 to 1879.

To describe her life—and as far as we may, her inner pilgrimage—we shall closely follow the witnesses, sometimes regretting that they were so discreet and that she had so little to say about herself. If we happen to advance a personal theory, we shall clearly state that we are doing so. We shall also do our best to present her life against the contemporary social history of her country.

We shall not burden the text with footnotes, even when trying to elucidate points of some complexity. The source material will be found listed at the end of each chapter. A critical evaluation of these sources is given in an appendix at the back of the book.

PART I

PREPARATION
(1792—1839)

Baptismal entry for Jeanne Jugan (Joucan) in the Cancale parish register.

1

CANCALE

(1792)

25 October 1792. In a cottage on the outskirts of Cancale, on the north coast of Brittany, a baby girl came into the world. That same day, she was baptised in the parish church and registered under the name Jeanne, daughter of Joseph Joucan[1] and Marie Horel[2], his wife.

Was the hamlet of Les Petites Croix delighted? Very possibly, but there were shadows too. The baby's father was away: a veteran sailor, he had sailed on 27 April for Newfoundland, for the fishing season. He was to return on 12 November, three weeks after the birth, but could anyone be sure he would return? The sea is a killer . . .

Then again, 1792 was a tragic year: the Revolution had broken out three years before, and now people lived in apprehension, if not in actual terror of their lives. The king was in prison, having tried to escape with his family. Soon, in 1793, the news would come that he had been sentenced and put to death.

The priests had been forced to choose between loyalty to the Pope and obedience to the law of their country; they

---

[1] Joseph Joucan, Jeanne's father, was born at Cancale on 26 March 1757. His name was variously written *Jouquan, Joucquan, Jouquand, Joucant*, but not *Jugan*. It was at Saint-Servan, where the name Jugan is common, that Jeanne's surname was corrupted into Jugan; and the new form stuck.

[2] Marie Horel was born on 22 July 1757. Her name was sometimes written *Horès*, but was in any case pronounced Hor-ay. She married Joseph Joucan, then a topsail-man, at Cancale on 29 April 1783.

3

had been compelled to subscribe the oath to the *Civil Constitution of the Clergy*, which Pope Pius VI had condemned. Those refusing to sign were obliged to go into hiding or into exile; many were arrested, massacred. The parishes were entrusted to the conforming clergy, and at Cancale the incumbent who baptised the infant Jeanne was Monsieur Godefroy, formerly a monk of Mont Saint-Michel.

Eventually the parish church was turned into a hospital, then into a fodder-store for the troops. Public worship was not resumed in it until 1802.

There was general discontent. No doubt, there was already secret talk of revolt, for the first incidents of the royalist and peasant rising known as *la Chouannerie* were to occur only a few months later. And from then on, for about the next eight years, bloodshed, repression, banditry and summary executions were to create such a climate of insecurity in Brittany as must inevitably have set its mark on the early childhood of Jeanne and her brother and sisters.

Jeanne was not the only, or even eldest, child of her parents. Five children had been born before her, but three had died in the cradle. She was greeted by a big sister of seven, Marie-Joseph (1785-1837) and a little brother, Louis-Julien (1790-1878) who was less than eighteen months old. Two other children were to be born later: Thérèse-Charlotte (1794-1881), 'daughter of Joseph Joucan, mariner, absent in the service of the Republic', and Gillette-Jeanne, also born during her father's absence (1796), who died when she was only two.

Absent for good, unfortunately. As early as April 1796, when Jeanne was three and a half, the register of seamen liable for service under the State noted of Joseph Joucan, 'Has not reported to the Recruiting Office. Said to have been drowned on a Cancale vessel.' He was to be long awaited. Seven years had to elapse before a man lost at sea was considered to be legally dead; but they went on hoping

much longer, since many French sailors had been taken
prisoner by the English. Was he one of these, perhaps?
Even as late as 1816, when Marie-Joseph got married, the
entry was to read, 'daughter of Joseph, absent for the last
eighteen years more or less, no word of him'. But that same
year, the five or six hundred Cancale men whom the
English had captured were repatriated; Joseph Joucan did
not return. The long wait must certainly have had a deep
effect on Marie Joucan and her children.

In Cancale, which was a town of seafarers, people were
prepared for situations of this sort. They understood the
sea. The men were often away; then one day the boat
would not come back, or would come back without them.
Thus, Jeanne's two brothers-in-law[3] were to die at sea, and
her brother, himself a sailor, was to take as his second wife,
in his old age, the widow of a sailor who had died in the
Newfoundland fishing-grounds.[4]

Unquestionably, the little girl born on 25 October 1792
knew how to laugh and have fun with her brother, sisters
and friends. But she grew up amid harsh events which
inevitably imprinted a certain gravity on her character. It
would be hard to say which had the more dramatic effect
on her: the Revolution or the sea.

[3] Guillaume Portier (1788–1818), Marie-Joseph's husband, 'drowned 14 October
1818, returning from Newfoundland', and Joseph Emery, Thérèse-Charlotte's
husband, who 'perished on 2 June 1826 in the wreck of the *Belle-Julie* on the ice
of the Newfoundland coast'. Marie-Joseph, widowed at 33, married secondly
Pierre-Marie Fauq.
[4] A pedigree of the Joucan family was drawn up by Henri-François Buffet (died
1973), Keeper of Archives for the Department of Ille-et-Vilaine. An expert on
Upper Brittany and its history, H-F. Buffet was particularly interested in Jeanne
Jugan and supervised much of the research about her.

SOURCES FOR CHAPTER 1

MANUSCRIPT SOURCES

Archives départementales d'Ille-et-Vilaine. In particular: *registres des Inscriptions maritimes* (before 1800).
Archives municipales de Cancale. Records of civil registration.
Archives paroissiales de Cancale. In particular: *livre de paroisse* (incumbency of Duval).
Archives des Inscriptions maritimes de Cancale. Registers.

STUDIES

F. Bouleuc, *Cancale, son origine et son histoire*, Cancale, 1886.

H.-F. Buffet, 'Le véritable nom de Jeanne Jugan', in *Bulletin de la Société d'Histoire et d'Archéologie de Bretagne*, 1952.

H.-F. Buffet, *En Haute-Bretagne*, Paris, Libr. Celtique, 1954.

J. Delumeau, *Histoire de la Bretagne*, Toulouse, Privat, 1969.

J. Vidalenc, *La société française de 1815 à 1848*, 2 vol., Paris, M. Rivière, 1970.

2

CHILDHOOD

(1792–about 1807)

In the eighteenth century, Cancale was famous for its oysters: the oyster trade employed a certain proportion of the population. Several dozen were sent off each week 'by mailcoach, for the King's mouth'. But they were not, as now, a special delicacy: in the coastal districts they formed part of the ordinary diet. And in the province of Brittany, where the diet was very poor, the abundance of shellfish and fish in general would seem partially to explain why the conscripts of Saint-Malo and Cancale were more robust at the beginning of the nineteenth century than men from inland!

Jeanne perhaps owed something of her physical stamina, which by any reckoning was considerable, to the resources she had drawn from her native place . . . All the same, hers was a poor home even before her father's death. The proceeds from fishing or from long sea voyages were often meagre. Further, it seems, Joseph Joucan had uncertain health. On 18 February 1793 we see him enlisting on a privateer—for the Republic had just declared war on England (1 February), and privateering then came back into favour. On enlistment, a sailor received three hundred francs advance pay;[1] but two months later, he discharged himself and presumably had to return the entire sum. On

---

[1] It is difficult to give today's equivalent, but apparently one could live very comfortably on a monthly income of 100 francs (or livres). Three hundred francs was thus a substantial sum.

3 August he enlisted in the National Navy and received 27
livres, but on 4 October he again presumably had to reim-
burse the advance since 'unfit to sail at this time'. He did,
however, sail the following 11 November, in *Les Trois Cou-
leurs*. His wife was left to feed the brood of four, and soon
five, children by her own efforts. As a girl, she had worked
on a farm: she went back to work by the day. She owned
a few animals herself, and Jeanne, who was still a child,
looked after the cows on the heights overlooking the bay of
Mont Saint-Michel, not far from Les Petites Croix. Before
she was much older, she knew how to spin wool and hemp
and to knit warm clothes. She learnt how to say the rosary.

Perhaps she liked to stand gazing out to sea, contemplating a sight ever new yet infinitely mysterious . . . She
must have steeped herself in those great seascapes, sometimes brilliant with light as when for instance you look
towards Cancale in spring from the opposite shore, with
the glitter of the intensely blue sea, dotted with white sails
between the pine-trees, the sheer rocks, the great sweeps
of blazing gorse; and sometimes dark and wild in storm,
when the high waves lash and roar against the jagged cliffs
of the Pointe du Grouin.

She would take the animals home, at evening time, shut
them in the small cowshed adjoining the house and once
more enjoy her mother's gentle affection in the big (and
only) room with its beaten-earth floor, where the family
lived. The Joucans rented the house[2] and Jeanne seems to
have loved it very much.

The town of Cancale itself was not rich at this period;
hunger often stalked its streets, and sometimes disease. In
1794, an epidemic broke out in a squadron in the roads.

[2] The house still exists. Owned by the Le Chapelier family and let until 1920 to
the descendants of Marie-Joseph, and then to the Guérin family, it was given in
1962 to the Little Sisters of the Poor, who restored it with the guidance of H-F.
Buffet, archivist of the Department of Ille-et-Vilaine. It is now a place of
pilgrimage.

Two thousand sailors died, and some townspeople later died as well. Recurrent dearths affecting the whole country were acutely felt in Cancale, especially during the terrible winter of 1794–5. Nowadays it is hard to imagine what these famines and their immediate effects were like with the gangs of (sometimes criminal) beggars roaming the countryside and spreading terror as they went.

There was no organised relief for these conditions. Fortunately, at Cancale people knew how to help one another. It is even related of the townswomen that, to help a neighbour who had no work, or who had just had a baby or recently been widowed, they made no bones about taking up a collection from house to house; this was so much the normal practice that it was not resented as a dole: whoever had money collected for her one day, knew that in given circumstances she would herself be out collecting for some-one else.

This experience of poverty, this austere sort of life, left their mark on the youthful Jeanne; as also perhaps this spontaneous and friendly money-collecting—mutual aid Cancale-style. Furthermore, mothers prepared their daughters to assume sole responsibility for the household in years to come, during the long absences or permanent absence of their husbands. It might one day be Jeanne's turn to do this, hence she had to learn to be strong.

Observing these confident, courageous, somewhat rough women around her, the child was struck by something else as well: she saw them pray, she saw her mother pray. Probably she quite often accompanied groups of these women as they set out, fasting and silent, at dawn, on pilgrimage to a little tumbledown chapel called the Chapel of the Sea, Our Lady of the Orchard. Its only feature was a plaster statue of the Virgin in an ivy-covered niche. This public act of worship was forbidden, but the commissaries of the Republic never succeeded in stopping the women from going and praying for their husbands and sons. Marie Joucan, who awaited her husband's return for twenty years, must certainly have taken part in these intercessions.

She talked about God to her children: she told them about the Gospel of Jesus and about sacred history. Organised catechism classes had been stopped. But many children in those days were secretly catechised by people living near them who had acquired a personal faith and a sense of responsibility as members of a sort of third order founded by St John Eudes in the seventeenth century. Spinsters or widows, they led their laywomen's lives as consecrated to Christ, always available for helping others, for instructing the young and for quickening faith. Although the convents had been suppressed, no one bothered about these *home-nuns*, these *trotting sisters* as they were called, who played an important role in handing on the Faith.[3] Despite successive waves of official persecution, and even during the period when the Pope, arrested on the orders of the Directory, was held prisoner and dying in France, the Gospel was patiently and discreetly handed on by these women. And it is not unlikely that, before joining the Society herself, Jeanne had received her knowledge of the Christian faith from it. She also probably learnt to read and write from the same source; her intellectual training was to go no further.

But more peaceful times were on the way. Towards the end of 1799, when Jeanne was seven, there was a perceptible easing of the tension. And on Easter Day 1802 the concordat signed between Bonaparte and Pius VII was solemnly proclaimed throughout the nation. Monsieur Alexis Met, who was a 'concordat priest', became incum-

---

[3] Strict conditions of admission and training notwithstanding, this 'Society of the Heart of the Admirable Mother' was very widespread: in 1859 it apparently had 6000 members in the diocese of Saint-Brieuc alone, and almost as many in the diocese of Rennes. See the *Manual* of the Society of the Heart of the Admirable Mother, published at Saint-Brieuc in 1859.

bent at Cancale; he was later to be remembered as a conscientious pastor and friend of the poor. The parish church was reopened for public worship.

It was presumably about then that Jeanne made her First Communion. On 8 November 1803, the Bishop of Rennes,[4] Mgr de Maillé, conferred the Sacrament of Confirmation on fifteen hundred people in the church of Saint-Servan: Jeanne perhaps was one of them.

At this point we owe the reader an explanation. In the course of this chapter we have put forward a number of conjectures: presumably, possibly, perhaps . . . the reason being that we have no document or personal reminiscence about Jeanne during her childhood. We only know of her from family traditions passed on in later years by her nieces the Emery sisters (the daughters of her sister Thérèse-Charlotte). They revered their aunt and repeated what their own mother had told them about her. These scraps of information are too slight for us to be able to describe her or indicate her good qualities or defects. Hence we have limited ourselves to this indirect testimony and to known historical facts concerning the period and region in which Jeanne was born. We have been careful—and shall be so throughout this study—only to present as fact what is solidly supported by reliable documents.

What, however, is not in doubt as regards Jeanne's childhood in her native cottage in the hamlet of Les Petites Croix is that she was poor, and very early imbued with the Christian faith.

---

[4] The diocese of Rennes was then only a bishopric. It became an archbishopric in 1859.

SOURCES FOR CHAPTER 2

MANUSCRIPT SOURCES

Archives départementales d'Ille-et-Vilaine. In particular: *registres des Inscriptions maritimes.*
Archives paroissiales de Saint-Servan. Registers.

PRINTED SOURCES CONTEMPORARY WITH JEANNE JUGAN

Règlement pour la société des Filles du Très-Saint Cœur de la Mère de Dieu, Dinan, Huart, 1825. Other editions: Caen, P. J. Yvon, 1757; Saint-Brieuc, 1859; Paris, 1914.

J.-M. Lécarlatte, *Essai historique sur les mouvements de Dol, le pays dolois,* etc., Paris, Hérold, 1864.

F. G. P. B. Manet, *De l'état ancien et de l'état actuel de la baie du Mont-Saint-Michel et de Cancale, des marais de Dol et de Châteauneuf,* etc., Saint-Malo, F. G. P. B. Manet, 1829.

LATER STUDIES

F. Bouleuc, op. cit.

H.-F. Buffet, *En Haute-Bretagne,* op. cit.

J. Delumeau, op. cit.

H. Devillers, *Les Cancalaises,* Paris, Floury, 1903.

C. de La Corbinière, *Jeanne Jugan et les Petites Sœurs des Pauvres,* Paris, Lecoffre, 1883.

C. Langlois and P. Wagret, *Structures religieuses et célibat féminin au XIX siècle, Les tiers ordres dans le diocèse de Vannes,* mimeograph, Lyon, Centre d'Histoire du catholicisme, 1972.

G. Turmel, *Cancale, Notre-Dame du Verger,* Dinan, Imprimerie commerciale, 1950.

3

LA METTRIE-AUX-CHOUETTES

(about 1808–16)

The term Malovian is applied to a type of mansion built
in the region of Saint-Malo during the eighteenth century
by rich shipowners or retired sea-captains of Saint-Malo as
comfortable family homes. Just such a house, four or five
kilometres from Les Petites Croix, in the commune of Saint-
Coulomb, was and is La Mettrie-aux-Chouettes. Despite
the name, with its somewhat sinister evocation of screech-
owls, there is nothing remotely sinister about the house,
indeed quite the reverse, as it is of remarkable elegance,
built in the classical manner, with its façade reflected in a
well-designed lake surrounded by magnificent trees. This
estate belonged to the family of La Choüe de La Mettrie.

Jeanne was engaged there as kitchen-maid, presumably
at the age of fifteen or sixteen, and she worked there for
several years. She arrived from her hamlet, a very timid
girl but willing to learn and to make a success of her new
job. Apparently the Vicomtesse de La Choüe received her
affectionately and behaved very considerately towards her:
she retained the habit, even long afterwards, of talking to
her in the familiar second person singular. Down the years,
she held her in the highest admiration. Jeanne's memory
remained alive and revered in this family.

For Jeanne was not only employed on kitchen work
there; gradually she became associated with the family in
relieving the poor. Receiving beggars, who came in large

13

numbers, was her job as kitchen-maid. But also, we may
suppose, visiting indigent families or lonely old folk with
Madame de La Chouë or on her behalf. There she early
learnt about sharing, about respect and tenderness. Being
poor herself and blessed with intuition, she must have
grasped something of the humiliation felt by the poor when
'being helped'.

It seems that she learnt something else from this family:
a certain refinement and a certain ease among the uses of
a world very different from her own. We shall see her
gradually growing more reflective, more attentive, more
sensitive. Now these were no doubt innate gifts, but they
seem to have been refined and encouraged to flower by
contact during her adolescence with an environment where
the art of human relationships had been cultivated for
centuries past. And she learnt to feel at ease with whoever
she happened to be talking to, whatever his or her degree
of culture or mode of expression.

The years went by. Jeanne became a woman. Can we
form a picture of what she looked like then? We know that
she was tall and thin. The only portrait of her, painted
very much later, may give us some idea of what she looked
like as a girl: regular, serious features, high cheek-bones,
lips ready to smile, a flame concentrated in her brown eyes.
A little later, her companions in the Marian congregation
at Saint-Servan considered her 'very pretty'. Our witness
for this impression did, it is true, qualify it by saying, 'no
doubt her modesty was the reason for this and made her
look beautiful to us.'

Anyhow, it was during these years that she caught the
eye of a Cancale lad, a young sailor, who asked her to
marry him. At the time in Cancale it was the custom for
a girl to choose her fiancé from a number of candidates
who declared themselves long before marriageable age. The
candidate made his intentions known when he was between

seventeen and twenty years old, then waited for two, three or four years before a final decision was made. Without discouraging this possible fiancé, Jeanne asked him to wait. And he waited.

During the years of the Empire, life had returned to normal, as though after a long winter; even more so, after the wars ending in the disaster of 1815. Historians, for instance, note signs of popular creativity, especially in Brittany. Spontaneously formed teams of local artists went round from church to church, repairing the damage caused by the Revolution and exercising a lively and vivid imagination. Similarly, cabinet-makers made and sold those fine pieces of furniture, tallboys and dressers, whose traditional characteristics imaginatively adapted still command our admiration. At Saint-Coulomb and Cancale, as elsewhere, this new sense of vitality must have made itself felt.

It also affected religious life, which experienced a great revival, especially after 1815. In particular, we see the vigorous spread of parish missions during this period. Thus, a mission was held at Cancale in 1816, conducted by no less than twenty priests; it lasted for three weeks; Jeanne attended the exercises, sermons and prayer-meetings. It is recorded of her that she was conspicuous for 'her recollection and fervour'.

It was perhaps an important stage in her interior development. In any case, at about this time her young man reappeared on the scene; this time, despite the faithfulness which he had shown, she gave him no hope at all. She had chosen to live the celibate life. God was calling her to his service.

On this occasion she said to her mother, 'God wants me for himself. He is keeping me for a work as yet unknown, for a work which is not yet founded.' On several other occasions she repeated these strange words in a grave tone of voice in her family's hearing.

Probably she herself did not really know what they meant; but thenceforth an obscure certainty lived in her heart. Many years were to go by before this call became specific.

Thus, and long in advance, she was preparing herself for a service about which she was to remain in ignorance for years to come. Little by little, she grew, her human gifts getting firmer and more refined, her faith becoming more lively. The fact of the matter was that God was slowly preparing her for the work for which he destined her in his Church.

SOURCES FOR CHAPTER 3

MANUSCRIPT SOURCES

Archives des Petites Sœurs des Pauvres. Letters of the Vicomte de La Mettrie.
Archives paroissiales de Cancale. Livre de paroisse (incumbency of Duval).

STUDIES

H. Devillers, op. cit.
A. Jardin and A.-J. Tudesq, *La France des notables, 1815–1848,* vol. 1, Paris, Seuil, 1973.
C. de La Corbinière, op. cit.

4

THE HOSPITAL OF LE ROSAIS

(1817–about 1823)

For the call to become clearer, it perhaps needed to be translated into action, into a departure, 'Go, leave your native land . . .' Aged twenty-five, Jeanne left Cancale.

The human reasons for this departure are unknown to us. Possibly the marriages of her two sisters had something to do with it. Marie-Joseph married Guillaume Portier on 8 April 1816, Thérèse-Charlotte married Joseph Emery on 16 June 1817. Jeanne had chosen a different way from her sisters. She was now a woman: better to separate and go their separate ways.

Besides, we may suppose that her sisters, although married, had not entirely left home, and possibly there was not overmuch room there. We shall in any case see two almost simultaneous births occurring in the hamlet of Les Petites Croix the following year—admittedly in the absence of the two fathers, both of them in Newfoundland. Françoise Emery came into the world there on 20 August 1818 at 6 o'clock in the evening, and Nicolas Portier on 21 August at 5 o'clock in the morning.

So, in the course of 1817, at the time of Thérèse-Charlotte's marriage or a little later, Jeanne announced her intention of leaving home: from then on, she would live on her own at Saint-Servan. It is recorded that, before leaving, she divided her clothes into two portions; she left her sisters 'everything she owned that was smart or pretty'; she was

17

going to live among and serve the poor; she wanted to be poor with them.

The parting seems to have been painful on both sides. The mother, brother and three sisters were devoted to one another. There were tears.

True, she was not going very far away and they could still see one another. Saint-Servan is only fifteen kilometres from Cancale. But there had never been a separation like this before. Jeanne was going away into the unknown, to face her own destiny.

Alone, reticent and proud, she walked away down the road towards Saint-Servan.

Arriving there with her little parcel of personal possessions, she may perhaps have noticed posters recently put up in the streets by order of the Municipal Council. They read as follows,

> The Mayor of Saint-Servan, considering that every day there appears in this commune a large number of vagrants of all ages and both sexes who besiege people's houses and snatch the alms due to the truly indigent; and that among this crowd of idle vagabonds there are some who, having displayed revolting sores to arouse pity in the beholder, or having annoyed them, go so far as to utter threats to force the hand of charity . . . Enacts as follows: . . . Article 2. A list of individual beggars shall be drawn up, whose absolute indigence is an attested fact. . . . These will temporarily be allowed to beg within the boundaries of the commune, though not elsewhere, and will clearly display a badge bearing the words 'Poor of Saint-Servan'. . . .

This official notice gives an idea of the situation. Saint-Servan contained a great many indigent families and beggars. A few years later, the Municipal Council was to count them: out of between nine and ten thousand inhabitants, the town contained 'four thousand persons reduced to begging their bread and receiving as much assistance as can be given by its Welfare Office and its hospital, which are far from adequate'. One can see why the commune had to be protected from bands of extraneous beggars coming in.

The same thing was true all over France, sorely tried during those very years by an acute shortage of grain. Not only had the harvest been very bad in 1816 and only middling in 1817 on account of the weather, but the effects were still being felt from the ravages and requisitions of the allied armies occupying France in 1815. The famine threw an immense number of poor people on to the roads, and their visits could be alarming. When a township organised a free distribution of bread, the poor had a feast—for bread was still virtually their exclusive diet. This was what happened at Saint-Servan on 25 August 1817 for the name day of King Louis XVIII.

So when Jeanne arrived in the town, she discovered a world of poor people in it to make her heart bleed. Forthwith she plunged herself into the very pit of all this misery by taking a job at the Hospital of Le Rosais.

Hospitals in those days were not at all like the ones we have today. They had more in common with the poorhouse or even with a prison than with a temple of medicine. To be admitted there was the last measure of despair when you were sick and without relations or resources.

The Hospital of Le Rosais—the only one in Saint-Servan—was styled the 'Civil and Naval Hospital'. It was staffed by a small group of Daughters of Wisdom and some twenty lay persons. In 1817 it admitted sixty sick civilians, two hundred and seventeen sick sailors, thirty-five foundling children. It had few resources, allocated by the municipality; it was very difficult to make ends meet. Even the food was often very insufficient. In 1818 a bakery was established in it, to produce cheap bread on a base of potato-flour.

This was where Jeanne went to work, with all her might

and also all her heart. It is recorded that her first job was the personal care of an infirm priest. Later she seems to have worked in the hospital pharmacy 'in a place where the preparation of remedies and medicaments could not be done correctly', the municipality having refused to put up a more suitable building. Later she served as a *nurse*—though of course without either the training or the competence that we should think necessary today. Two little *jugs* have been preserved which, it is said, she used to use for making herbal infusions. It is also related that she took advantage of her free moments to take a male nurse aside and teach him the catechism; her sense of apostolate, we see, was already aroused.

The work was rough and hard: in the deliberations of the administrative committee, there are frequent references to patients suffering from 'scurvy, itch and venereal disease', who had to be looked after. In 1820, owing to lack of funds, the staff was further reduced and the food rations cut.

Jeanne seems to have outworked her strength. After about six years at the hospital, she was completely exhausted and had to leave.

She had learnt a great deal there, about human nature and about medicine. She had served and loved the poor, the sick, the aged; she had gained experience of the techniques then in use—though rudimentary indeed, they were later to be useful to her. And many years afterwards, in her old age, she was to teach young novices the correct art of making 'infusions, herbal teas and cataplasms'. Above all, she had gained the experience of a total commitment of self.

These first years at Saint-Servan were decisive in another way; there Jeanne experienced a deepening of her faith, and this we must deal with next.

SOURCES FOR CHAPTER 4

MANUSCRIPT SOURCES

Archives des Petites Sœurs des Pauvres. Testimony of Little Sisters of the Poor: Sœur Ignace de Sainte Marie, Sœur Joseph de Sainte Hermance. Other testimony: Sœur Victor-Marie de Montfort (Daughter of Wisdom).

Archives municipales de Cancale. Records of civil registration.

Archives municipales de Saint-Servan. Deliberations of the Municipal Council; Mayor's correspondence; documents concerning the Hospital of Le Rosais.

Archives de l'hôpital du Rosais. Deliberations of the Administration Committee of the Hospital of Le Rosais; registers.

STUDIES

G. Foligne (Doctor), *Contribution à l'histoire hospitalière de l'agglomération de Saint-Malo.* Thesis for doctorate of medicine, mimeograph, Rennes, 13 January 1969.

A. Jardin and A.-J. Tudesq, op. cit.

C. de La Corbinière, op. cit.

J. Vidalenc, op. cit.

5

THE THIRD ORDER
OF THE HEART OF MARY

The mission at Cancale in 1816 had marked an important
stage in Jeanne's life. Shortly after her arrival at Saint-
Servan, at the end of 1817, she took part in another mission
which lasted for five weeks. A group of 'Fathers of the Faith
of Jesus'—Jesuits, that is to say, who had not yet reassumed their name—conducted it. They were anxious,
there as elsewhere, not to let the religious revival die down
once the mission was over, and to this end they suggested
that those people of Saint-Servan who were willing should
group themselves into Marian congregations. This was a
feature of Christian revivalism at the time. On 8 December,
the Fathers publicly announced that they hoped to establish three congregations: 'one for men and boys, another
for wives and widows, and the third for young persons of
the Sex' (i.e. young girls). We know that Jeanne joined this
latter group, the members of which undertook to pray to
Our Lady, to live a true life of faith and to take part in the
assemblies of the Christian community.

Her friends of those years preserved the memory of the
processions at Corpus Christi and the feast of the Assump-
tion, in which they all took part. Some of them found her
very austere, and used to say, 'Let's not get too close to
poor old Jeanne Jugan. She doesn't *get herself up* properly
for these great feasts. She would disgrace us.' Not that she
neglected her appearance; quite the opposite, they empha-

The cottage occupied by Joseph Joucan's family in the hamlet of Les Petites Croix, on the road from Cancale to Saint-Malo (see Chapter 1)

The principal room, where Jeanne was born during the night of 24–5 October 1792—*Photo Jean Fortier*

Le Rosais, 'Civil and Na
Hospital', Saint-Servan,
where Jeanne worked fro
1817 to about 1823 (see
Chapter 4)—*Photo Petites
Soeurs des Pauvres*

The house in the rue du Centre,
Saint-Servan, where Jeanne and
Françoise Aubert took a flat over-
looking the courtyard in 1837 (see
Chapter 7)

Kitchen in the flat in the rue du Centre. The ladder leads to the loft, where Jeanne slept after giving her bed to Anne Chauvin (see Chapters 7 and 9)—*Photo Jos Le Doaré*

Montyon medal awarded to Jeanne by the French Academy in 1845 (see Chapter 14)—*Photo Jean Fortier*

The first house opened by Jeanne in Rennes, in 1846, in the suburbs of La Madeleine (now rue de Nantes). The building has recently been demolished (see Chapter 16)

Chapel of the Jesuit College, Rennes. Jeanne and her companions worshipped at the parish church of All Saints from 1846 to 1852 (see Chapter 16)—*Archives départementales d'Ille-et-Vilaine.*

sised that she was 'of irreproachable cleanliness and modesty', but it seems that those early years at Saint-Servan were characterised by a certain radicalism in her determination to follow Jesus. She had chosen poverty and was not afraid to express this choice even in the way she dressed.

At about this time, she had furthermore decided to give her life a more definitely consecrated character than that of merely belonging to a Marian congregation; she entered the Eudist Third Order, the Society of the Heart of the Admirable Mother which we have already mentioned in Chapter 2.

In point of fact, no written document directly proves that Jeanne Jugan belonged to this society. There is, however, a certain amount of evidence which allows it to be taken as certain. The importance of the point requires that we should devote some space to it.

First, a very firm and uncontested tradition avers that Jeanne was a Eudist tertiary.

Next, her earliest biographer, the Abbé Leroy, whose critical honesty was extreme, accepted this tradition as well founded. The documents on which he evidently relied have now disappeared with his personal papers (see Appendix), but we know from other sources that he made it his principle to discount traditional affirmations which did not strike him as having adequate documentary support.[1]

In 1895, the Abbé Collet, who had been curate at Saint-Servan in 1849 and had known Jeanne Jugan well, stated

---

[1] Sister Marie de la Croix (Joséphine James), archivist of the Congregation of the Saints Cœurs de Jésus et de Marie, of Paramé, notes specifically in connection with Jeanne Jugan's membership of the Third Order, 'We knew the learned and holy priest [the Abbé Leroy] well and we knew that he would never have approved a matter of this importance without having been very sure; for when he wrote the history of our own Congregation, we saw him leave out certain facts for lack of adequate documentation.'

unhesitatingly that she was a tertiary at Saint-Servan in 1839.[2]

Other testimony: that of a former tertiary at Saint-Servan, Eugénie Gautier, who stated that her own sister, also a tertiary, and eight years older than herself, had known Jeanne in the Third Order when their group used to meet in the bell-tower of the church (later, an interesting detail, their meetings were held in the house of the Little Sisters of the Poor).[3]

The Congregation founded by Jeanne preserved the memory of the vow of chastity pronounced by her first three companions on 15 August 1842; Jeanne herself did not need to make this promise, since she had already taken a vow of celibacy for the sake of the Gospel: tertiaries would take this vow.

Finally, the little rule drawn up in 1842 for the first associates shows such similarities to the rule of the tertiaries as cannot be accidental. Now, Marie and Virginie were too young to enter the Third Order; the age required was twenty-five years. Only Jeanne, then, could have contributed these basic elements; and how could she have known them if she had not herself been practising them as a tertiary?

We do not know at what date she became one, but it cannot have been before 25 October 1817, the date of her twenty-fifth birthday.

The members of the Third Order led a form of religious life at home. They met regularly for communal prayer and reflection. They followed a rule of life and a timetable of daily prayer. Each year they made a retreat for several days. We know, for instance, that on 15 October 1825 two hundred and fifty-five of them met for a retreat in the

[2] A. Helleu, *Note sur le travail de l'abbé Leroy*, p. 9.
[3] Testimony gathered by Sister Marie de la Croix (Joséphine James), letter of 30 January 1936.

'Maison du Rocher' at Saint-Servan. It is very likely that
Jeanne Jugan was one of them.

Priests helped them, under the direction of the Superior-
General of the Eudists. Thus, the Abbé Sauvage, who had
been Jeanne's confessor—she first knew him when he was
a curate at Saint-Servan—later became chaplain to the
'Maison du Rocher' and received many groups of tertiaries
there.[4]

It was no mere set of observances that the tertiaries
found in the tradition of their society, but the call to a
Christianity of the heart, the invitation to a free and personal faith, a living relationship with Jesus Christ.

If we open the *Manual*, such as Jeanne Jugan must have
held, we find that everything in it is based on Baptism: the
tertiaries frequently called their baptismal vows to mind;
each year they made 'an act of renewal of their Baptism
and consecration' (Chapter 17).

Here is a passage from their Act of Self-dedication:

> O Mother of Love, I give you my heart and freedom entirely
> and without reserve; fix it so mightily to the Divine Will that
> I am obliged, cost me what it may, to obey it everywhere in
> all things; and unite my heart so closely to the Heart of my
> Jesus, of which yours is the perfect image, that I have no other
> feelings, affections or wishes than yours . . . (Chapter 15)

A very interior, very spiritual adhesion to the Love which
comes into the world to renew it. In the same spirit, the
rule lays down, 'We should always have a small crucifix
about our person; we should take it in our hands, kiss it,
meditate on it; and He will speak to our hearts' (Reflections
on the Habit).

The only thing that counts for them is love. Their desire
is to have their hearts free enough truly to love, 'They will
try to live at a distance from and in general indifference to,

[4] He died of cholera there on 19 October 1848.

what is not God,' for perfect love 'cannot endure any sharing of the heart' (Chapter 5). Although they will not neglect exterior mortification, 'they will apply themselves more to interior mortification, that is to say, to the abnegation of their own will' (Chapter 7). The way of interior freedom.

This way also makes them free with regard to exterior ceremonies; a 'true daughter of the Most Holy Heart of Mary . . . does not insist on going to church, to religious ceremonies, when her presence is needed elsewhere.' 'Of a tender and active charity reaching out wherever it can,' in the very name of their loving relationship with Jesus, they make a point of assuring a loving and attentive presence to others; in particular, they love 'the poor, the simple, because Jesus Christ and the Blessed Virgin loved them' (Chapter 17). And the rule lists various types of mutual assistance which they can practise.

And lastly, they are to try and love one another like the early Christians. 'All members of the Society will have great openness of heart and cordiality one for another, so that the early spirit of Christianity may be seen as renewed in them' (Chapter 6).

We have insisted on the spirit of the Third Order—the very spirit of St John Eudes—since we believe that it had a profound influence on Jeanne Jugan. There essentially she found the secret of her inner strength and inner freedom. She lived according to it throughout the long period of her life as a laywoman, and later—as we shall see—she was to share it with the young women who became her companions in the 1840s. This was one of the currents which contributed to creating the spirit of the Little Sisters of the Poor.

The *Manual* of the Society invited its members to mutual spiritual and material aid, 'especially when someone is sick' (Chapter 6). And see, here is Jeanne Jugan quite worn out after some six years of back-breaking work at the Hospital of Le Rosais. She was to be taken in, looked after and loved by an excellent woman, Marie Lecoq, who, tradition tells us, was also a tertiary of the Heart of Mary.

Title page of the Rule of the Third Order of the Heart of Mary
(see Chapter 5).

SOURCES FOR CHAPTER 5

MANUSCRIPT SOURCES

Archives des Petites Sœurs des Pauvres. Testimony: Abbé Collet reported by Abbé Leroy, Eugénie Gautier reported by Sœur Marie de la Croix (J. James).

Letters or notes: Père Jégo (Eudist), Sœur Marie de la Croix (J. James). *Notes sur le travail de l'abbé Leroy.*

Archives de l'Académie française. Mémoire des habitants de la commune de Paramé réclamant un Prix Montyon en faveur de Mlle Fristel Amélie Virginie. Paramé, 1854.

Archives de la maison du Rocher, à Saint-Servan. Historical account of the 'Maison du Rocher'.

STUDIES

C. de La Corbinière, op. cit.

C. Langlois, op. cit.

G. Lefebvre, Ch. Pouthas, M. Beaumont, *Histoire de la France pour tous les Français,* vol. II, Paris, Hachette, 1950.

A. Leroy, *Histoire des Petites Sœurs des Pauvres,* Paris, Poussielgue, 1902.

6

MADEMOISELLE LECOQ

(about 1823–35)

Jeanne Jugan—for so she was henceforth to be known, the people of Saint-Servan having substituted Jugan for her real name, Joucan, as more familiar to them—in about 1823, Jeanne Jugan then went to lodge with Mademoiselle Lecoq (1772–1835) who was twenty years her senior. She took the job as her maid; but more than a servant, she became her mistress's protegée and friend. Mlle Lecoq was the sister of a priest who had refused to subscribe to the Civil Constitution of the Clergy and died in 1805; she lived at Saint-Servan, in the rue du Centre, almost opposite the church. The people of Saint-Servan long retained the memory of Mlle Lecoq and her companion and their regular sisterly attendance at the services of the parish church. It was said of her that she was 'completely absorbed in good works'. Although badly off, she cheerfully shared in a hidden way with those worse off than herself. For the next twelve years, Mlle Lecoq and Jeanne were to practise this ministry of sharing.

But first of all, poor Jeanne had to be got better. With somewhat anxious tenderness, Mlle Lecoq set about the task. She shielded her, nursed her, pampered her. The stairs in the house were steep and gave Jeanne palpitations. Mlle Lecoq forbade her to carry even the smallest burden up to their flat on the second floor. If Mlle Lecoq saw her looking a little drawn, 'Quick, quick, Jeanne!' she would

29

say, 'you are *completely worn out!*' and insist on her taking *white sugar*. Jeanne was evidently thoroughly run down, and her poor state of health seems to have made her nervous about herself. Anyhow, she consented to take things easy, and to do the Stations of the Cross in church, carrying a chair to sit on.

During this period was she tempted to become pre-occupied with herself, to think too much about her own health? If so, nothing indicates that she ever succumbed to the temptation.

Mlle Lecoq's charitable activities undoubtedly helped, by keeping her in contact with the sufferings of others. As also did the atmosphere of prayer and apostolic zeal of the little community which they themselves composed. They prayed together, they read spiritual books to each other and attended Mass every day; they talked freely about God. Jeanne contributed to creating this atmosphere by spontaneously giving voice to the act of thanksgiving already always ringing in her heart. It is related of her that if she happened to burn her fingers in the kitchen, she would say in a half-humorous way—which we shall under-stand better later on—'Blessed be God!' or 'Thank you, my God!'

Together they taught the catechism to the children of the parish. Jeanne was specially responsible for the periods of recreation; she used to make the children sing hymns. She used to put all her heart into this, and sometimes Mlle Lecoq had to intervene, 'She would have gone on till she had no strength left.' With the children, with the poor, with the people she met, Jeanne displayed a gentleness and evenness of temper impressing them and winning her everyone's affection.

We are told nothing about her relationship with her family, whom she had left at Cancale, but it seems certain that the death of her brother-in-law Joseph Emery, news of which must have reached her towards the end of the summer of 1826, when the wreck of the *Belle-Julie* was announced, came as a blow to her and occasioned a family reunion.

There were also the events and disasters of the world at large. True, she was not likely to be much interested in political life as such, and it is worth remembering that at the time in question only a restricted number of people were interested in it. First, because in the 1820s, two thirds of the adult population were illiterate (though this was not the case with her); secondly, because newspapers were not sold individually in those days, and a regular subscription was very expensive[1]; there were not more than sixty thousand subscribers in the whole of France. And finally, because the electoral qualification restricted the right to vote to a very small number of wealthy people, and then only to men; in Ille-et-Vilaine, even after 1830, there were still only eleven hundred and thirty-nine people with the right to vote, out of a population of more than half a million! Public affairs were the business of a fairly small ruling class, the great body of the population virtually playing no part.

But the great upheavals in national life inevitably affected Jeanne, particularly those of the years 1825–32. In 1825, there was a serious economic crisis in London, which had repercussions in France, then in the early days of industrialisation. The years 1826–9 were marked by bad potato crops, just as the potato was beginning to form an important component in popular diet; and there was a cereal shortage in the years 1827–30. Once again, roving bands of more or less aggressive kind, made up of unemployed farm labourers and factory workers, were to be seen; hunger became more acute in the towns. If the July Revo-

[1] About 80 francs of the time.

lution of 1830 passed almost unnoticed in Brittany, the troublous conditions of those years—riots, acts of arson in the countryside and so forth—must certainly have made themselves felt there. It is in fact said that this province gave the Government particular grounds for alarm and that this hastened the installation of the optic telegraph between Avranches and Nantes by way of Rennes, which we shall mention again in the course of this book.[2]

Many towns found themselves with an increased number of indigent people on their hands. Such was the case at Saint-Servan. In February 1832, a commission presented the Municipal Council with a report on 'the elimination of begging', a common expression of the day, when people seem to have had difficulty in diagnosing the causes of the situation. As a result of this report, an organisation was set up by an 'Administrative Committee for Welfare', its president being the mayor, and its vice-president, the parish priest. The town was divided into eighteen wards, in each of which two ladies were responsible for discovering the most deserving cases and distributing assistance to them. It is very possible that Mlle Lecoq formed part of this network. But it is certain that she and her companion were indirectly affected by it and collaborated with it, since they were already active in working for the poor.

Had they, one wonders, heard of a young Parisian student of the day who succeeded in canalising a great deal of available charity into an organisation for helping and sharing? Frédéric Ozanam founded the Society of St Vincent de Paul in Paris in 1833. Probably his name had not reached Saint-Servan at the time of these humble beginnings; later, the movement initiated by him was to encoun-

---

[2] The optic telegraph (Chappe) consisted of a chain of semaphores, built on the tops of hills or on towers, by which messages were transmitted. The electric telegraph (Morse) was not invented until 1837 and came into common use much later.

ter and reinforce the stream of charity shortly to be released
by Jeanne Jugan.

But dear Mlle Lecoq was not much longer for this world.
Aged only sixty-three, she fell ill, and it soon became
apparent that there was no hope for her. Jeanne warned
her, helped her to prepare for death and receive the Sacraments. On 27 June 1835, she performed the final service
of closing her eyelids.

We can well imagine what sad days these were for her.

Her mistress and friend bequeathed her her entire estate:
her furniture and a small sum of money which, added to
her own savings, amounted to 600 francs.

These twelve years, humanly speaking, seem to have
been among the pleasantest of her life, a breathing-space
as it were before choosing her new road and setting forth
into the blue with no return.

But in this summer of 1835 God had still not clearly
shown Jeanne what path she was to take. It was to take
another four years for the radical decision to mature, of
which the Lord had given her a glimpse in her girlhood.

For the time being, Jeanne was alone once more. What
should she do?

SOURCES FOR CHAPTER 6

MANUSCRIPT SOURCES

*Archives de l'Académie française. Mémoire adressé par la commune de
Saint-Servan pour solliciter l'attribution du Prix Montyon en faveur de
Jeanne Jugan.* 1844.

Archives municipales de Cancale. Records of civil registration.

Archives municipales de Saint-Servan. Deliberations of the Municipal Council; records of civil registration.

PRINTED SOURCES CONTEMPORARY WITH JEANNE JUGAN

The article by the English tourist : see Chapter 17.

LATER STUDIES

H.-F. Buffet, *Le véritable nom de Jeanne Jugan*, art. cit.

J. Delumeau, op. cit.

L. Dumolin, 'Jeanne Jugan, première quêteuse des Petites Sœurs des Pauvres'; in *Les Contemporains*, no. 362 (17 September 1899), Paris, Bonne Presse.

A. Jardin, A.-J. Tudesq, op. cit.

C. de La Corbinière, op. cit.

J. Lefebvre, Ch. Pouthas, M. Beaumont, op. cit.

Dictionnaire de Théologie catholique (Letouzey and Ané), art. *Ozanam* (Frédéric).

7

JEANNE,
FANCHON AND VIRGINIE

(1835–9)

In the autumn of 1835, Jeanne reached her forty-third year. She had to earn her living. It seems that she tried to get a job as a maid in a house in the district, possibly at Saint-Malo; but she did not stay. Why not? We do not know.

Anyhow she decided to live at home and earn her living by working on a daily basis for various people in Saint-Servan or thereabouts: housework, washing, or, whenever she could, nursing. She was a *nurse*, after all!

She established a lasting relationship with a number of these people and their families, and later we shall see her renewing contact with them; they were to be friends and props of Jeanne and her poor. Thus, in later times we shall keep coming across the families of Tréhouart de Beaulieu, de Gouyon de Beaufort, Leroy, de Kervers, Citré, with whom she became acquainted then.

Madame Citré had a grocer's shop in the Place de la Paroisse; her daughters, especially Anne, were friends to Jeanne. Jeanne did housework by the day for them. She also used to go round the town selling curds, that is to say, curdled milk cooked and put into scallop-shells (*coquilles Saint-Jacques*); 'Curds, who wants curds?' she would cry in a hoarse, weak voice. The street urchins used to copy her merrily, repeating in a piping voice, 'Curds, curds! Hurry up or Jeanne will be dead!' Anne Citré related that her friend would exhort her to live in thanksgiving for and despite everything, 'In our joys, in our troubles, in the contempt that others show us, we must always say, "Thank you, my God, or Glory to God." '

For some time, Jeanne had had a friendly relationship with a woman considerably older than herself: Françoise Aubert (1766–1850), familiarly known as Fanchon. The latter had long been in service with a priest of Saint-Servan, who at his death had left her a small income.

In the course of the year 1837, the two of them joined forces and rented a flat: two rooms on the second floor of a house in the rue du Centre. Jeanne thus went on living in the quarter of the town where she had lived so long with Marie Lecoq, quite close to the church. Upstairs, there were another two rooms made in the roof, to which access was had by a trapdoor. There they lived the common life to the rhythm of prayer: a life not very different from that formerly shared with Mlle Lecoq, except that both of them now had to earn their own living. Fanchon did spinning at home; Jeanne continued to work by the day, outside.

But soon a third person was to join them: a young girl of seventeen called Virginie Trédaniel (1821–53). An orphan whose father had been lost at sea, she was the ward of one of the municipal councillors of Saint-Servan, Edouard Gouazon, whose idea it was to entrust her to Jeanne. She seems to have had no problem in entering the prayerful life of her two seniors. From 1838, all three of them—aged seventy-two, forty-six and seventeen—were to lead a regular common life, which only death was to interrupt.

Jeanne for her part regularly attended the meetings of the Third Order and continued to honour her promises. It is not unlikely that, with Amélie Fristel (foundress of the Congregation of the Saints Cœurs de Jésus et de Marie, of Paramé), she attended the retreats conducted in 1837–9 by

Father Jérôme Louïs de la Morinière, the Superior-General of the Eudists.

She continued her activities in the world of the poor, whom she encountered endlessly in the streets of Saint-Servan: many known and well-loved faces, and so many others whom she would have liked to help. Long afterwards it was recalled at Saint-Servan how, when she happened to meet one of the aged poor carrying a bucket of water, she would say, 'Have you far to go with that?' and very often carry the bucket herself. When dealing with the indigent, she would find out what their particular needs were, frequently taking steps on their behalf or bringing them what they needed.

As regards this problem of indigence, the commune of Saint-Servan was struggling against overwhelming odds. At the meeting of the Municipal Council of 4 February 1836,

> those present forcefully expressed their resentment at the alarming rise in the rates which the citizens have to pay this year, insofar as this affects the poorer class, depriving them of several days' food . . . Saint-Servan, comprising some ten thousand souls, contains no more than six hundred families in reasonably easy circumstances.

On 16 February 1839,

> the Superior of the Sisters attached to the Welfare Office urgently asks for an augmented grant for the poor, whose number is considerable and whose circumstances at present are exceptionally cruel.

Jeanne knew this herself; she felt it. But what was to be done? Above all, she found the situation of the aged poor, forsaken, often without help or hope, particularly heart-rending. An enormous problem, completely beyond her . . .

But was it enough to be wounded to the heart? Shouldn't she allow herself to be wounded in her flesh as well? Should she not, in a kind of madness, even share the necessities of life, even share her home? Wouldn't that really be loving?

Such were the questions probably running through her mind in the wintry weather of December 1839. The answer was to come of its own accord in the ravaged and pleading face of a poor old blind woman: for Jeanne, this was to be, as it were, an irresistible sign.

SOURCES FOR CHAPTER 7

MANUSCRIPT SOURCES

Archives des Petites Sœurs des Pauvres. Testimony: Eugénie Vosluisant.

Archives des Sœurs des Saints Cœurs, de Paramé. Correspondence of Fr de la Morinière.

Archives municipales de Saint-Servan. Deliberations of the Municipal Council; Mayor's correspondence.

STUDIES

H.-F. Buffet, *En Haute-Bretagne,* op. cit.
C. de La Corbinière, op. cit.
A. Leroy, op. cit.

8

JEANNE AT FORTY-SEVEN

At the moment when Jeanne was to take the decisive step committing her beyond return, she had already travelled a long road: she had forty-seven years of living behind her.

We have seen her born in the often tragic context of the French Revolution and of dramas at sea; her family were poor and devout. As an adolescent, she had worked as a maid in a mansion where she acquired a degree of refinement and early learnt to serve the poor—humbly. After this, she left home to devote herself to caring for the sick poor in the hospital at Saint-Servan, a town where great poverty was to be found. There she joined the Third Order of the Heart of Mary, the strong free spirituality of which focused her on the essential of religion: a living relationship with Jesus Christ. After a few years of exhausting work, she was taken in and made much of by kind Mlle Lecoq: a time for pausing and waiting. But the poor whom she served there, too, kept calling to her. Left on her own, she sought her way. Eventually she let that call take her over completely. She linked her fate once and for all to that of the aged poor.

At this point can we already foresee some of the characteristics of what will be Jeanne Jugan's *spirituality*?

Two axes are already well defined, or rather two poles of the same magnetic field: God and the poor.

God, known and loved in Jesus, sought in prayer, present every moment of life as watchful, attentive love. She

responds to him by thanksgiving and joy, which are already
permeating her entire existence; and also by often renewed
act of choice, by renunciation of all self-centredness, in
communion with Jesus, to do the Father's will.

The poor, members of Jesus, specially loved by God,
demand respect and loving attention, demand to be listened to and served; and in her we already see the desire
to be with them and share their deprivation, the better to
love them.

Jeanne already knows, and has for a long time known,
that God is calling her to consecrate herself to him; and
she foresees more and more clearly that she will have to
live out this consecration in the humble service of the poor.

By various stages, notably her departure for Saint-Servan and her membership of the Third Order, her certainty
about this has long been maturing in the depths of her
heart. Finally it bursts into bloom that day when, at the
onset of winter, 1839, Jeanne Jugan gives up her bed to
the poor old blind woman, Anne Chauvin.

PART II

FRUITFULNESS

(1839–52)

9

THE FIRST AGED WOMEN

(1839–41)

Towards the end of 1839, possibly in the first cold days of winter, Jeanne said goodbye to her employers the Leroys, where she had been working for a long time, 'I am not leaving you to take another job. I intend to devote myself to charitable work. Every day when I go to the market, I see poor destitute old women.' Monsieur Leroy seems to have then asked her how she proposed to feed them. 'I shall go collecting,' she replied, 'and I shall begin with you. I know you won't refuse me!' And he gave her three hundred francs on the spot.

And a few days later, certainly with Fanchon's and Virginie's approval, she took an old woman home with her. Anne Chauvin (the widow Haneau), who was blind and infirm. Until then, the latter had been assisted by her sister, but the sister had fallen ill and had been taken to hospital, Anne now found herself abandoned. It is related that to get her up the narrow stairs of the house, Jeanne carried her on her back. What is certain is that she gave her her own bed and herself moved into the loft. And she 'adopts her as her mother'.

Shortly afterwards another old woman, Isabelle Cœuru, joined Anne Chauvin. She had served her old masters to the end; these having fallen on hard times, she had spent all her own savings on them and then gone out begging to keep them alive. When they died, she was left worn out

43

and infirm. Jeanne heard this impressive story of faithfulness and sharing; thanks to her, it would be repeated, with
many another, to the ends of the earth! Joyfully, without
delay, she took her in. This time, Virginie was the one to
give up her bed and move into the loft.

At night, having made their two patients comfortable
and said goodnight to honest Fanchon, Jeanne and Virginie
would climb up their ladder and, taking off their shoes so
as not to make any noise, would finish off their work and
say their prayers; Jeanne related this memory herself.

All three of them worked (Virginie was a dressmaker) to
feed and support five people, two of whom were old and
sick; sometimes they had to stay up late at night to do the
mending or the washing.

It may have been even at this stage that Jeanne had
recourse to well-disposed people, who were later to become
her regular benefactors. The Tréhouart de Beaulieu family
preserved the memory of her visits. When she had taken
her first 'good woman' in—for such was the expression,
used in no demeaning sense—they remonstrated with her
in a friendly way; but she took no notice and ended by
getting what she wanted. She went back again, having
taken in the second—more remonstrations. Jeanne sat
quite unmoved, 'Madame Trouhart (for so she pronounced
the name), I shan't go away until you have given me
something, if only a few spuds and the crusts from the little
girl's lunch!' And she danced the little girl of four or five
up and down on her knee, making her laugh by wrapping
her up in her big hooded cloak (the outer garment worn
by the peasant women of the day). She made a habit of
visiting this well-disposed family once a week.

Virginie had a friend of about the same age as herself,
called Marie Jamet (1820–93), who very soon became
acquainted with the household in the rue du Centre. She
herself lived with her parents in Lambéty (nowadays part

of Saint-Servan); her father was a mason, and Marie worked with her mother, who kept a small shop.

She often came to the rue du Centre of an evening and 'in this place, so dear to her heart, would spend the rare moments she could call her own, as also her Sundays.' Gradually, Jeanne, too, became her friend. And all three of them—sometimes, with Fanchon, all four—would talk of God, of the poor and of the questions which life presented. Marie and Virginie knew that Jeanne belonged to the Third Order of the Heart of Mary; they themselves were too young to join it, but they conceived the idea of giving a certain direction to their lives by adopting a sort of personal rule to follow in common to bring them nearer to Jeanne. She helped them do this, explaining the essentials of the tertiaries' rule of life which she had long been following on her own account. Consequently, the little rule adopted by the two friends closely resembled that of the Third Order.

It is worth spending a few moments in comparing the two texts. The vocabulary, it is true, is not the same (it seems, in fact, that the tertiaries' handbook was not allowed to be lent: Jeanne's friends thus did not have access to it). Several specific points, however, are very close, and certain typical expressions occur in both. Thus, in each, during the morning and afternoon, a time of recollection and silence is envisaged; the drafting of the various spiritual exercises is very similar; there is insistence here and there on sacrificing one's own will; and there is much about 'hiding in' or 'withdrawing spiritually into' the Heart of Jesus; the invitation to help children, the sick, the poor, is very similar. So a common inspiration is not in doubt.

Often, on Sundays, Marie and Virginie would go for a walk together. They would stop, on the shore, in a cranny among the rocks which they had discovered, and there they would talk long about their lives, their plans and their faithfulness to God, reviewing the way they were keeping the rule of life which they had given themselves.

They also discussed these matters with a young curate who had recently arrived in Saint-Servan and whom they had both chosen as their confessor, the Abbé Auguste Le Pailleur (1812–95). He encouraged their spiritual friendship and gave his approval to their rule.

They also talked to him about Jeanne and about the poor women whom she had so lovingly taken in. So much so, indeed, that he, too, began to take an interest in their work. Enterprising, ingenious and able, he also was concerned about the poor; he thought it right for him to support a work which might grow into something bigger.

He himself came one day—15 October 1840—to where Jeanne was living; possibly he climbed into the loft. There he presided over a meeting of the three friends and there together they decided to create a charitable association, the rule of which would be precisely that little rule worked out for Marie and Virginie. Feeling too old, Françoise Aubert was to remain outside, not the shared friendship, but the association and the promises made in common.

Jeanne was probably delighted with the help brought by this young priest. He was not her confessor, but approved of her somewhat mad scheme and was prepared to help.

In December, the little flat, already pretty full, took in another, sixth, person, a young working-woman of twenty-seven who was very sick and had expressed a wish to be nursed by Jeanne. Thinking that she was about to die, she intended to leave her few possessions to the poor, to Jeanne's poor. The latter took her in and nursed her. She recovered.

Thenceforth, Madeleine Bourges (1813–83)—for that was her name—formed part of Jeanne's group. She went back to live in the room which her employers had left her in gratitude for her good work (she was a washerwoman) but used to come to the rue du Centre as often as possible to give all the help she could. By stages, she was to join the association and become one of its active members.

In the course of the present chapter we have witnessed two decisive events, inseparable the one from the other. The one: by giving up her bed to Anne Chauvin, Jeanne had taken the redoubtable step leading her out of a very rational existence into the extravagance of love. The other: a group had been formed, never to be dissolved, forming the embryo of the Congregation of the Little Sisters of the Poor.

SOURCES FOR CHAPTER 9

MANUSCRIPT SOURCES

Archives des Petites Sœurs des Pauvres. Testimony of Little Sisters of the Poor: Marie Jamet reported by Sœur Alexis de Sainte Thérèse, Sœur Alexis de Sainte Thérèse, Sœur Sainte Mélitine, Sœur Alphonse de la Nativité, Sœur Léonce de la Nativité.

Other testimony: Mme Godbert, Mlle Kervern. Little Rule of 1840.

Archives de l'Académie française. Mémoire pour l'attribution du Prix Montyon à Jeanne Jugan.

Archives municipales de Saint-Servan. Records of civil registration.

PRINTED SOURCES CONTEMPORARY WITH JEANNE JUGAN

Règlement pour la société des Filles du Très-Saint Cœur . . . op. cit.

STUDIES

C. de La Corbinière, op. cit.
A. Leroy, op. cit.

10

THE 'BIG DOWNSTAIRS'

(1841–2)

Jeanne Jugan's two lodgers, Anne Chauvin and Isabelle Cœuru, soon recovered their health and zest for life. But there were many, many others still outside! The thought of all these haunted Jeanne and she passed her anxiety on to her companions.

Couldn't they take in others as well? But first of all, what were they to live on? It was hard enough already with five. But Jeanne was not prepared to be put off by this objection. Within her, she felt so strongly moved to come to these poor people's help that it was as though God's own love were invading her heart. Yes, with a kind of obscure certainty she felt that this would be God's work, love's work, and that, if she put her trust in him, all would be possible. But the other objection was a more serious one: the house was full and there was no way of stretching the walls!

So the associates simply decided to move house. This took place in the summer of 1841. A lease was available on some premises not far from the rue du Centre, on the way down to the Solidor harbour: a former bar with a large, low room, admittedly rather damp and very dark but where there was easily room for a dozen beds. At the far end, a little room could be used to accommodate the associates, although at very close quarters; and another would serve for keeping the stores and doing the rough work. All this could be had for one hundred francs a year. They clinched the deal.

They moved in at Michaelmas, their five wooden beds, two cupboards, the table, a few chairs, all being carried down on litters. Jeanne, Fanchon, Virginie and the two old women moved into the rue de la Fontaine, and the same day four other old women came to join them; a month later there were twelve of them. Monsieur de Bonteville, the recently appointed parish priest of Saint-Servan, came and blessed the house and its inhabitants.

One room was lacking. Where could Jeanne and her friends meet to pray in peace? There was no loft, as in the rue du Centre. A neighbour, Madame Mignot, lent them a room in her house: this was their oratory.

They divided the work between them. Françoise, who was already seventy-five, took charge of the housekeeping.

Virginie gave her wages and also helped with the house-work, often late into the night. Madeleine continued to do laundering, or did spinning at home. Marie, who was still living with her parents, for her part ran a small vegetable business and contributed the profits. Jeanne, who took a hand in everything, was mainly concerned with activities outside.

On Sundays, they took those of the old women who could walk to the parish Mass: already quite an imposing group and passably disabled, and a not altogether welcome sight to everyone as they took their seats in church. Although there was a good deal of sympathy, there was already some fairly sharp criticism too.

Sometimes they had visitors. One day, a girl came in accompanied by her little sister, Irma and Clémentine Le Fer de La Motte. The child, later to be known as Madame de La Corbinière, to whom we are indebted for valuable recollections about Jeanne, left an account of her visit. Her sister and godmother had said to her, 'God-daughter, I'm going to take you to see the *Jeanne Jugans*.' They then went into

> *a big downstairs room* (i.e. on the ground-floor) where seats were
> few but the beds, in contrast, were very close together, and I
> made myself small [she relates] on a stool between two cots,
> the blankets of which were made up of a countless number of
> scraps. I saw . . . Jeanne Jugan; she greeted the two visitors,
> that is to say, my godmother and me, with a kind smile and
> a little curtsey: that was all, because she was getting ready to
> go out collecting; she was putting on her cloak and adjusting
> her hood. Over her arm she put her basket, already such a
> well-known sight all over the town . . . The old women called
> her Sister Jeanne. 'Sister Jeanne,' they would say, 'do our job
> properly for us, collect for us, don't forget our errands, our
> tobacco and our pennies.' Jeanne would lean over them, lis-
> tening to a few more whispered instructions; she smiled at
> them. I am fairly sure she kissed one or two of the old
> women—the blind ones perhaps. She left them promptly, for
> she did things quickly, yet never giving the impression of
> hurrying or being hurried. I was impressed by the cleanliness
> reigning in this large, rather dark room, and also by the way
> the poor furniture was arranged. [On leaving, her sister said
> to her] Did you notice how well those old women are being
> looked after and how happy they look?

This is an attractive and lively picture of Jeanne serving
her old friends. Many other witnesses have emphasised her
smiling affection. She would do the impossible to please
the aged, even in their whims, and this sometimes took a
great deal of patience!

On another occasion, the visitors were a certain Monsieur Bosquet, a shipowner who had known Jeanne at Le
Rosais, and the Abbé Portier, one of the Saint-Servan curates. They were collecting money in that part of the town
and came in by chance. Monsieur Bosquet was so touched
that he gave all the money he had on him. And over supper
in the presbytery, the Abbé Portier related, 'Monsieur Bos-

quet and I have come across something extraordinary: two poor spinsters have given shelter to twelve old women whom they feed and for whom they go round the houses collecting left-overs.'

Another visit: by her nieces, her sister Thérèse-Charlotte Emery's daughters. These adolescents asked her, not without some disdain, why she *gathered up all those old women*. To which, in an icy and very unfamiliar tone of voice which they were never to forget, she replied, 'Those old women had been forsaken. I am giving them a home!'

We have already noted that Madeleine Bourges used to spin—presumably wool or hemp. The old women who could, used to spin too. The idea was to sell part of this woollen or hempen thread. In Brittany, this was the normal thing to do. People did a lot of spinning and weaving. Packmen, at least until 1850, used to travel France selling Brittany-made cloth. So, for the poor community, here was one modest source of income. And besides, Jeanne had sensed that work has a rejuvenating effect on the aged; today's occupational therapy exploits this same truth.

Jeanne Jugan's work was now well known in Saint-Servan. And requests would often arrive: could you possibly take in such-and-such a person who is destitute? She had to refuse; it was not possible to get one more bed in. They had only spent three months in these dismal premises when they were already beginning to think about having a larger, more convenient house. It so happened that part of a former convent, suppressed and confiscated by the State some time before, was up for sale: the house of the Daughters of the Cross, quite close to the church. To buy it, the considerable sum of twenty thousand francs had to be found: could this be done? Yes, if the poor needed it. Jeanne gave all her savings, publicised the scheme and began tapping the generosity of the people of Saint-Servan and Saint-Malo. A tradeswoman of her acquaintance called

Mademoiselle Doynel agreed to take part in the operation. The Abbé Le Pailleur sold his chalice and gold watch. Eventually, on 5 February 1842, Mlle Doynel and the Abbé Le Pailleur, whose parish priest had recently made him officially responsible for the work, acting jointly on behalf of the association, acquired the former convent. It was hoped that Jeanne's collections would succeed in extinguishing the debt: 12 000 francs to be got together by Michaelmas . . . and 8000 over the following seven years.

At about the same time, Virginie Trédaniel left *the big downstairs* and the common life for a few months: it was thought that, with an eye to the future, she should acquire a smattering of education. The nuns of Montauban-de-Bretagne had agreed to take her in and give her some training.

For they were already thinking about the future, even while immersing themselves in the rude tasks of the present; they were getting organised and trying to progress. On 29 May 1842 (the feast of Corpus Christi), the association held a meeting after vespers, the Abbé Le Pailleur being present. Virginie was not there; whereas Mlle Doynel, who was then considering joining the group, did take part in the meeting.

Marie and Madeleine chose Jeanne as superior and promised obedience to her. (Virginie was to make the same promise later, on 10 July.) The associates took a name: they called themselves *Servants of the Poor*.

Into their rule of life they inserted a few new practices of obedience, poverty and modesty. Father Félix Massot, of the convent of St John of God at Dinan, had been much impressed by Jeanne and her companions. His experience of the hospitaller life and his various advice on prayer and loving the Cross, were a great support to them.

Thus Jeanne and her companions embarked, henceforth without return, on a charitable work, the law of which was already to share the distress and penury of those whom they sought to help, to be with them in their poverty and to strive to get out of it together. And this appears very clearly in the decision to go begging for the poor.

SOURCES FOR CHAPTER 10

MANUSCRIPT SOURCES

Archives des Petites Sœurs des Pauvres. Testimony of Little Sisters of the Poor : Sœur Alexis de Sainte Thérèse.

Other testimony : Mlle Bosquet de Linclays, Mme Lavoué. A. Leroy, *Détails complémentaires se rapportant à 'Histoire et Œuvre des Petites Sœurs des Pauvres'.* Legal documents.

Archives de l'Académie française. Mémoire, op. cit.

Archives de l'hôpital du Rosais. Deliberations of the Administrative Committee.

STUDIES

P. Dauphin, *Vie de M. l'abbé Hay de Bonteville,* Paris, Mersch, 1888.

J. Delumeau, op. cit.

C. de La Corbinière, op. cit.

A. Leroy, op. cit.

11

BEGGING FOR THE POOR

'Sister Jeanne, go out instead of us, beg for us.' This was what the old women said. By this they emphasised the very heart of this activity of begging. Jeanne substituted herself for the poor, identified herself with them; or rather, guided by the Spirit of Jesus, she recognised that the poor were her 'own flesh' (Is 58:7). Their distress was her distress, their begging was her begging. This was how God loved us in Jesus.

Practical considerations led her to do the begging herself: if she had allowed the *good women* to go the rounds of the town, as they used to before she had given them shelter, she would have exposed them to many evils, especially those of them who were given to drink. So, she respectfully asked each to give her the addresses of her benefactors and then did the rounds herself instead. She used to explain, 'Well, sir, the little old woman won't be coming any more. I shall be coming instead. Please be so kind as to go on giving us your alms.' Note the *us*.

It was not an easy decision to take. Jeanne was proud; in spite of knowing how admirably the women of Cancale came to one another's help, this was not sufficient to make her cheerfully take to begging. In her old age, she would still recall the victory over self which this had frequently required. 'I used to go out with my basket, looking for something for our poor . . . It cost me a lot to do this, but I did it for God and our dear poor.'

In this she was helped by a Brother of St John of God,
Claude-Marie Gandet (1806–84). The Brothers of St John
of God at that time had a fervent community at Dinan and
also a hospital. They were to play an important part in
Jeanne Jugan's search for the right methods to adopt. Was
Brother Gandet's visit the first contact she had with them?
He himself was collecting for the Brothers' hospital when
he knocked at Jeanne's door; he found her extremely per-
plexed. They understood each other, and he helped her
make the deliberate choice of going out to beg. To encourage her, he promised to support her and introduce her to
a number of families whom he himself used to visit. It is
even said that he presented her with her first begging
basket. We have already mentioned another of the Brothers, whom we shall often meet again in the course of this
book: Félix Massot, who was to give Jeanne a great deal
of help in drawing up the rule of the Little Sisters. This
man was a spiritual giant who contributed much to the
restoration of his Order in France. The very humble beginnings of Jeanne's work reminded him of the beginnings of
his own Order in Granada. It is certain that, from this
year 1842, they contracted a confident and friendly
relationship.

So Jeanne began to go begging. She asked for money,
but also for gifts in kind: food—the remains of meals or
left-overs were often particularly appreciated—things,
clothes. 'I should be very grateful if you could give me a
spoonful of salt or a small piece of butter.' 'We could do
with a copper for boiling the sheets.' 'A little wool or filasse
(i.e. hemp) would be useful to us.' She was not shy of
putting into words what she lived by faith. If she happened
to be asking for some wood to make a bed, she would be
specific and say, 'I should like a little wood to relieve a
member of Jesus Christ.' She accepted whatever she was
given. Later she was to advise the novices, 'Never throw

anything away that comes by way of begging, until you have seen if you can't find some use for it.' One day, in the village of La Froulerie, a gardener who knew about the adventure to which she had just committed herself, said, 'Jeanne, what are we to call you now?' 'The humble servant of the poor.' 'Then, this way please, humble servant of the poor!' and he gave her some vegetables.

She was not always so well received. In the course of one round, she rang a rich and miserly old man's doorbell. Knowing how to get on the right side of him, she persuaded him to give her a good contribution. Next day, she called again. This time, he was angry. She smiled, 'But, sir, my poor were hungry yesterday, they are hungry again today, and tomorrow they will be hungry too.' He gave again, and promised to go on giving. Thus, with a smile, she knew how to invite the rich to think again and discover their responsibilities.

Sometimes she was treated as a cadger. 'Why don't you go and do an honest day's work?' 'I do this for my poor, sir.' Many times, she was turned away; she said, 'Thank you.' 'You're mad to say thank-you when shown the door.' 'It's for God.'

One incident has become famous. An irritable old bachelor struck her. Gently she replied, 'Thank you; that was for me. Now please give me something for my poor!'

She often used to apply for help at the Welfare Office and in the early days she was treated as a member of the organisation. But one day a woman employee was rude to her and told her to take her place in the queue with the beggars. She obeyed. She was a beggar after all, it was the right place for her.

She was careful never to make any comment about those who had given her a bad reception. This was the advice she used to give the young when she was old herself,

There will be people who will swear at you and send you away. The neighbours will say, 'You had a very poor reception next door,' but you must never show resentment. Whenever this happened to me, I used to say, 'Oh no, those people treated me very well.' For, you see, when we are given a hostile reception, this is good for us and something we can offer to God.

Even her friends would reproach her from time to time. Mme de La Mettrie, her old employer who was very fond of her, would say, 'My dear Jeanne, you weigh yourself down with this horde of old people. You can't feed them! Our resources are limited, I have four children. What with your old folk, you'll reduce us to sleeping on the floor!' She never answered back, and went on as before.

Sometimes things went badly. Then she would drum up her courage. She would say to her companion, 'Let's go on for God!' Or, one feast day at Saint-Servan, with one of those half-smiles characteristic of her, 'Today, we're going to make a good collection. Our old folk have had a good dinner, so St Joseph ought to be pleased at seeing his dependants being well looked after. He is going to bless us!'

It seems she had a quality of presence which impressed people, and a sort of charm which worked on them. Many people of different walks of life bore witness to this.

In the early days of the foundation, [the grand-daughter of one of her benefactors reports] she continued to go out working by the day. Before starting her foundation she was not particularly demanding, but once she had taken in her first *good women* she became insatiable. Espying some trinkets, she said to my grandfather, 'My dear sir, these are no use to you, you would be just as happy without them. If you gave them to me, I should sell them, and my poor could live for quite a long time on the money which I should get for them.' Of course, my grandfather kept the trinkets and gave her the money. She was so expert at begging and did it so nicely and so tenaciously that it was really impossible to refuse her.

Her 'tenacity' was always courteous, discreet, ready to step aside. Later, her advice was to be, 'Be careful not to *rush* your collecting and not to blurt out what you want as soon as you open your mouth as though it were your due. Take time to say good-morning and, if appropriate, to say a few words to show your interest in the people themselves and in what is going on. This is more humble, and less pressing. Then gently explain the needs of the house, but do not be wearisome.' Or again, 'Be very little, very humble, and don't look up at the windows, if they don't answer the door at once!'

Mme de La Corbinière records memories which may well have been her own.

The servants, having answered the door, took no further notice of her. Jeanne would slip quietly down the passage, knocking discreetly at one door after another, patiently waiting, since she was afraid of being a nuisance. In the drawingroom, in the scullery, in the garden, Jeanne would make her appearance in the same gentle, quiet, persuasive way. Immersed in his affairs, the banker would look up and see Jeanne standing motionless before him, waiting for the favourable moment. 'Well, Jeanne, what are you doing here?' 'I am waiting, sir. I am collecting for my women.' 'Your women? I don't know why you've lumbered yourself with them. Are you trying to lumber me with them too?' 'We shall share them between us today, sir, if you will be so kind. You will feed them and I shall look after them. Give me a nice lot and you won't see me again for a long time. I shall pray for you, sir. They too will pray for their benefactor. I shall make sure that they are grateful.'

She did her collecting with dignity, at once avoiding any suggestion of arrogance or of servility. One witness of her visits records,

When I was a child, what struck me most forcefully was her gratitude, her way of saying thank-you and her even expression, whether people gave or refused. 'Jeanne,' I would say, 'Mummy has sent me to tell you that there is nothing for you today.' 'I see, thank you, miss, thank you all the same. That will be for another time. Thank your Mummy kindly. I know she would like to fill my basket if she could.' Jeanne never failed to drop a little curtsey before leaving us.

She always said thank-you, and this was an expression of a truly heartfelt gratitude. Besides, she was thanking God at the same time as thanking her benefactors; she blessed him for the slightest gift received, even if only one potato! 'This is why God always blessed me,' she was to confide many years later, 'because I was always thankful to Providence.'

Léon Aubineau, who knew Jeanne well, records her indefatigable zeal in collecting and the incredible results which she obtained. And he has this delightful formula, 'She had a gift for speech, a grace in asking . . . she collected by praising God, you might say.'

Conducted thus, collecting became transfigured. It might have aroused a simple reaction of giving, by which rich people could salve their consciences; but Jeanne made it a work of evangelisation, causing people to search their consciences and encouraging a change of heart.

This evangelistic purity was not understood by everyone and many of the people of Saint-Servan did not care for it. They were ready to seize on any ground for complaint that could be levelled against her. When the purchase of the Maison de la Croix became known, a whole movement sprang into being to oppose this mad adventure; such a work ought to be entrusted to experienced religious, or alternatively to a committee of ladies which had recently been formed to open a foundlings' home; they could support it and run it at the same time. How could an enterprise like this be left in the unaided hands of an illiterate maid with no money?

The parish priest of Saint-Servan, Monsieur de Bonteville, thought fit to refer the matter to Mgr Brossais St-Marc, the recently appointed Bishop of Rennes. The latter upheld Jeanne's cause.

But public opinion was still uneasy. The Welfare Office withdrew its support forthwith: there would be no more clothing, bread or any other assistance for Jeanne's refuge in future.

The loss of the clothing was felt most. They were very short of it and there seemed no way of getting any. They set to praying even harder. It was in August; they set up a little altar in the house in honour of the Virgin; a neighbour, Monsieur Brisart, a policeman by calling, and very skilled with his hands, made it for them. Friends gave flowers. It had been planned that Marie, Virginie and Madeleine would take a six-months' vow of chastity that day (Jeanne had already done this long before); they made their vow as planned and, taking off their rings and earrings, adorned the statue of the Virgin with them. On the altar, they put what little clothing they had left, and said this prayer, 'Kind Mother, look on our distress! We have no clothing to give your children a change of clothes.' In the days following, charitable people laid a considerable amount of clothing at the foot of the altar, and even a whole bolt of cloth.

The stay in the *big downstairs* was drawing to an end. The closing days were marked by two encouraging events. First, Fr Félix Massot of the Brothers of St John of God presented Jeanne with an act of union of prayers and graces between his Order for the one part, and for the other the Abbé Le Pailleur and 'Jeanne Jugan, Superior of the young persons consecrated to the care of the infirm aged in the parish of Saint-Servan'.[1]

This recognition of the work undertaken, which Jeanne must surely have seen as a delicate expression of friendship and brotherly support, was followed by another: on 27 September, two days before they moved house, the Bishop himself paid a visit to the little community. This official action rallied the sympathies of many Saint-Servan people who had previously been dubious about Jeanne Jugan's work.

After his visit, Jeanne could breathe more freely: the storm was over. Rather like returning from certain collecting-rounds, as she came back heavily laden, with tired feet. Then she would sit down for a moment at the foot of a large Calvary standing out in the country and catch her breath. Above her, the Lord's Cross unveiled the meaning of the life she led. Love is primarily a sharing in the world's distress.

SOURCES FOR CHAPTER 11

MANUSCRIPT SOURCES

Archives des Petites Sœurs des Pauvres. Testimony of Little Sisters of the Poor : Sœur Anne Auguste reported by Sœur Anne de la Nativité, Sœur Isabelle de Saint Paul reported by Sœur Alexis de Sainte Thérèse, Sœur Emmanuel Marie reported by Sœur Valentine Joseph, Sœur Marie Gatienne reported by Sœur Léocadie Marie, Sœur Anatolie du Saint Sacrement, Sœur Apollinaire du Saint Sacrement, Sœur Armel du Saint Sacrement,

---

[1] This is the original Latin text: *Dilectissimo in Christo Domino admodum reverendo Patri Le Pailleur sacerdoti, simul ac Dominae reverendae Matri et Matronae Joannae Jugan superiori puellarum infirmis utriusque sexus senio confectis inservientium in parochia Sancti Servatii. . . etc.*

A French translation annexed to this act of union actually reads, 'To the Reverend Mother and Lady Jeanne Jugan, Superior *General* . . .' We shall have more to say about the transformations which this official diploma was to undergo.

Sœur Auguste Alexis, Sœur Catherine de tous les Saints, Sœur Céline de l'Ascension, Sœur Geneviève Monique, Sœur Louise de l'Immaculée, Sœur Marguerite de Sainte Marie, Sœur Pélagie de la Résurrection, Sœur Sainte Amélie, Sœur Saint Aurélien, Sœur Sainte Laurentine, Sœur Saint Michel.

Other testimony: Mme Delamare reported by Mme Salles, Mme Gillet reported by Sœur Louise de l'Immaculée, Mme de Beaudrap, Mlle de Kervers, Vicomte de La Mettrie, Mme Magon, Mme de Molon, M. Moncoq, Mme de Senneville.

Diplôme d'union de prières avec l'Ordre hospitalier des Frères de Saint-Jean-de-Dieu. Affidavit of F. Durusselle, Vicar General of Diocese of Rennes (1902). *Livre de fondation* of the Saint-Servan house.

Archives de l'Académie française. Mémoire, op. cit.

Archives de l'Ordre des Frères de Saint-Jean-de-Dieu. P. Pierre-Fourrier Picard, *Souvenirs épars de nos religieux défunts*, *Notice nécrologique du P. Félix Massot*.

PRINTED SOURCES CONTEMPORARY WITH JEANNE JUGAN

L. Aubineau, *Histoire des Petites Sœurs des Pauvres,* in *Les serviteurs de Dieu,* 5th ed., Paris, Palmé, 1880.

LATER STUDIES

Frère Corentin (Cousson), 'Jeanne Jugan et les Frères de Saint-Jean-de-Dieu' in *La Grenade,* September 1939.

P. Dauphin, op. cit.

H. Devillers, op. cit.

A. Helleu, *Une grande Bretonne, Jeanne Jugan, fondatrice des Petites Sœurs des Pauvres,* Rennes, Riou-Reuzé, 1938.

C. de La Corbinière, op. cit.

A. Leroy, op. cit.

12

THE MAISON DE LA CROIX

(1842–5)

'It is a disgrace to our civilisation when you think that, in the nineteenth century, one tenth of the population is in rags and dying of hunger.' And what is the reason for this? The reason is that

> industry is a machine functioning without a regulator and heedless of the driving-power it uses. Indifferently grinding up men and material in its wheels, depopulating the country-side, crowding people into airless slums, weakening the spirit and body alike and ultimately, when having no further use for them, throwing on to the street those who have sacrificed their strength, their youth, their very existence to create industrial wealth.

The author of this pitiless analysis was not some revolutionary, but Prince Louis-Napoléon Bonaparte, then reflecting on social conditions before in turn accepting political responsibility. His tract, from which these lines are quoted, is entitled *The Suppression of Pauperism (1844)*.

Jeanne was not to read it: she read the book of life as life presented it to her. She had no clear understanding of the causes of pauperism, but she found a way of remedying it where she happened to be; she threw in her lot with that of the aged poor and from this chosen position addressed the human community around her, 'Do you want us to go on living? Our lives depend on you.' And for those prepared to listen, this question could lead on to all the others.

Let us watch her at work.

Thus, at Michaelmas 1842, less than three years after taking in the first two *good women*, Jeanne, her companions and the twelve inmates left the old bar where they had been living for the past year and moved back up the street into a real house at last: quite spacious premises built round a courtyard. The same day, another six old women joined them. There was room there for a proper dormitory and also space for the community.

Beds were made out of old church benches (no doubt the honest Brisart had a hand in the carpentry). The old benches were also used for making other pieces of furniture—and for firewood.

The number of inmates was about to rise steeply. More hands were needed for all the work. Madeleine Bourges gave up her room and came to live at the Maison de la Croix. She and Virginie Trédaniel stopped doing outside work: all their time thenceforth was to be devoted to the poor (but this meant that there was that much less income coming in). Shortly afterwards, Marie Jamet joined them: leaving her parents' home, she came to devote herself full time to the same service.

In November, the home for the aged admitted twenty-six old women. Some of them were sick. Jeanne could no longer nurse them on her own. Then, Monsieur Blachier, a doctor at Le Rosais Hospital since 1806, who thus knew Jeanne well, agreed to give free treatment to the aged sick. From then on until 1857, he was to show immense devotion to them. He it was who set up a small pharmacy for the home.

The problem of clothing arose again. The new arrivals were often covered in vermin and had to be completely reclothed; and on occasion the Sisters had to give up their own clothes to dress them in. A bit later, since there was nothing to change into and since cleanliness demanded it, the washing had to be done during the night. While the clothes were drying during the daytime, the old women had to stay in bed; this caused some discontent. Jeanne and Marie made a grand clothing collection throughout the town and restocked the home.

An important event occurred during this winter of 1842–3: the admission of the first old man. Jeanne's attention had been drawn to an old sailor, alone and sick in a damp cellar; she went to see him and found him in a most deplorable state, in rags, on rotten straw, haggard of face. Moved by liveliest compassion, Jeanne went off, confided to a charitable acquaintance what she had just seen, and came back a moment later with a shirt and clean clothes. She washed him, changed his clothes for him and took him back to the house. There he was to recover his strength. He was called Rodolphe Laisné (1767–1849). Other men were shortly to join him there.

Since, from then on, Jeanne had a reputation for accepting anyone who was in trouble, people began bringing her foundlings too. It even seems that she may have taken the initiative in admitting them, at least as a temporary measure; much later she was to relate how one day when out collecting and walking along a hedge out in the country, she heard a child crying; she stopped, took the child with her and brought it back to the home. Thus, for about five years, there were ten or so children at the Maison de la Croix; we shall have more to say about this.

It was a very poor life they led, economising even on heat and light. If someone had to sit up with the sick, this was done in the dark, the candle being lit only when necessary. One evening after the poor had been given their supper, all that was left for the four Sisters was 'a penny roll'. They shared this but it did not go far: the day's labours weighed heavily on them. Then, at about 8 o'clock, the boy from the presbytery brought the remains of a meal.

There were tears—and the Sisters dined.

And here perhaps is the place to tell this meaty anecdote. From time to time, Jeanne would have little adventures which filled her with that pure joy known to those who serve the Lord. She dreamed of giving her old folk a treat. Or to speak more plainly: she wanted to get some bacon and, by the same token, to buy a pig.

Paramé fair was about to be held. Jeanne Jugan asked Mlle Anne Citré to go to it with her; the latter agreed in her usual good-natured way . . . Our two friends looked the animals over, bargaining nervously, buying nothing. Plainly, no animal's price was going to be reduced to the modest figure that Jeanne could offer. Time went by . . . Our would-be buyers had their heads together, arguing gently in an undertone. Anne Citré was scolding Jeanne, and the latter was counting up the little she had and sighing to see the beast she coveted, but could not afford, being carried off before her eyes. They were getting ready to leave when they were hailed by a market-woman who had been observing their antics and timid behaviour from a distance, 'This way, this way, ladies, I've got just the thing for you. I've sold the rest of the litter and now I've only got one left. But, word of a Dinard woman, I've sworn not to take anything home with me. Here you are, look at it.' The beast was lame, sickly, consumptive-looking, in a word unsaleable. 'All it wants is a fair chance,' she went on. 'The other piglets ate its rations and jealousy has done the rest! Reared on its own, it will fill your larder all right!' Bored and overtired, Anne Citré said to Jeanne Jugan, 'Take it—as a present from me. That will put a stop to your havering. Here's the money. We'll give the animal a tonic as soon as we get home to Saint-Servan.' They paid for the beast and set off for home. The way led across the fields and marshes. At one point there was a bridge to cross. For fear the pig should come to grief or be drowned, Jeanne put the animal into the big bag (the big *pochon*[1] as she called it) carried for any eventuality. But halfway over the bridge, moans broke out. *'It's groaning in its poke,'* said poor Jeanne, 'I think it's dying.' They stopped and opened the bag. The creature was at its last gasp. Dead-eyed, limp-eared, dumb: such was the poor beast that now had to be carried in their arms with all possible care like a sick baby.

When they finally got home, Anne Citré administered the tonic aforesaid, which worked wonders. Thenceforth the pig gave nothing but satisfaction and fair hope. Its death, when this finally occurred, was a day of rejoicing for the household. It weighed two hundred pounds.

The two friends, as usual, made light of their exhaustion, yet they may indeed have said with a smile—so one of their companions asserted to Maxime du Camp, 'It wouldn't matter in the slightest, if we could only have new pairs of legs.'

They learned to rely on Providence. Thus, a debt of six hundred francs was almost due and they only had thirty francs left in the cash-box. They prayed. And precisely on the date required, a local priest presented the home with a roll of gold coins to the value of four hundred francs.

Jeanne went on collecting indefatigably. Unexpected help came forward. A certain Mademoiselle Dubois, a friend of the house, offered to go collecting with her in the neighbouring villages. She was a woman of some social standing, which she compromised by going begging with Jeanne. Her presence caught people's imagination and untied their purse-strings. They were given wheat, buckwheat, potatoes, and then thread and cloth, and new friendships were built up. They collected left-overs more assiduously than ever. They began collecting in markets and, in the port of Saint-Malo, at the ships. In buying the

---

[1] *Pochon* is a word still in use in Brittany and a few other parts of France, Champagne for instance, to denote a sack or bag.

Maison de la Croix in February 1842, they incurred the heavy debt of twenty thousand francs; by the end of 1844, with seven years still in hand, Jeanne had paid off the lot.

They were constantly thinking of new ways to bring in an income. At Christmas in the year 1842, for instance, they made a large crib taking up one entire room in the house. This was the joint work of several friendly families: Gouyon, Guibert, Chatelier, Le Fer. The girls dressed the shepherds and wise men; the boys built palaces for Herod and Pilate. Crowds of people came to see and the offerings were considerable: the seven to eight hundred francs thus brought in went to pay for the kitchen stove. On another occasion, there was a lottery, also organised by benefactors' families.

Another new idea: they bought crude wool and bleached it. The *good women* carded it, spun it and knitted it. And Madeleine would go round the villages, selling the knit-wear, sometimes with oddments bought in bulk at Rennes or Dinan.

Thus they lived from hand to mouth. Never in advance. And it was no small matter for surprise in the district to see the poor, of whom there were more and more, being well looked after and happy, although the home had no assured income. Only the communal effort of the whole town, ceaselessly stimulated by Jeanne, could produce such a result.

There were collective efforts too. For instance, the work-men at the Guibert shipbuilding yards arranged among themselves, as from February 1843, to contribute a penny a week per head (there were several hundred of them), and this collaboration lasted for several years.

In December 1843, the Maison de la Croix admitted forty indigent people, the majority of them plucked from beggary; in 1845, there were to be more than sixty. Many became reformed characters, and people told one another about this in astonishment. Like the poor old woman who used to go rag-picking through the streets and inspired the whole town with a kind of horror. After a few months in the home, no one would have known her for the same person. Or there was the former fishwife who had taken to drink; gradually giving up her work, she took to begging and wandering along the shore, a pitiful sight. Relations who were better off had helped her but to no purpose. The Sisters took her in, surrounded her with affection, and she was completely changed. One of her nephews, Monsieur Lapanouse of Jersey, came to see her. Declaring it a miracle, he forthwith bequeathed seven thousand francs to the Sisters of the Poor—and died shortly afterwards.

This sum came at exactly the right moment. For they had in fact started to enlarge the house: what an act of folly! There were only fifty centimes in the cash-box: they put the coin at the foot of the statue of the Virgin and set to work! The Sisters themselves brought back stones under their cloaks; when the pile was large enough, they dug a bit of sand out of their garden. Then they opened a public subscription, which was well supported. They got free cartage, building materials at reduced prices, and a little money—enough to make a start. Masons and carpenters offered a day's work a week. The Sisters themselves puddled the lime and sand. The walls rose from the earth. The seven thousand francs from Monsieur Lapanouse allowed them to get as far as the roof-timbers. At this point, there was no money left. So they waited. In December 1845, three thousand francs came in from the Prix Montyon, which paid for the completion of the building. But that is another story, to which we shall come in due course.

Meanwhile they had furnished one large room as a chapel, and permission had been received to reserve the Blessed Sacrament in it. On 10 April 1845, the Bishop visited the Maison de la Croix and conferred the Sacrament of Confirmation on ten of the aged.

Another visitor has left a description of some aspects of the house at this period. This was Monsieur Dupont, often known as 'the holy man of Tours' (1797–1876), whom we shall encounter on other pages of this story. Born in Martinique, he came as a widowed magistrate to France with his only daughter. Her health was frail, he brought her to Saint-Servan for the sea-bathing (this was the very beginning of summer holidaying on the Breton beaches). Deeply devout, he loved devout Brittany. And he met Jeanne Jugan, was enchanted by her; and a deep sort of affinity sprang up between them. This was what he wrote from Saint-Servan on 17 September 1844, 'A small detached building houses the old men, of whom there are far fewer. In coastal towns, male mortality is higher, men being exposed to the perils of the sea.' He then described the

> room where the women assemble to unpick old rope to make oakum for caulking the ships. The room is large and square in shape, with chairs along all four walls. Complete silence reigns and a sweet serenity plays on every face. . . . It has taken great effort to bring each of these poor creatures, whom society had rejected and whose conduct was frequently bad . . . to this regular, hard-working way of life. . . . One's admiration is redoubled when one reflects that this good order has been brought about by the agency of five or six young women. . . . The finger of God is in it.

The finger of God is in it. The Sisters themselves had learnt to recognise this during those early years at the Maison de la Croix. Starting from nothing, they progressed with nothing. Since they were doing God's work, God would provide for their needs—for the needs of his poor. Such was the law of trust, henceforth to be the great law of the Little Sisters of the Poor.

SOURCES FOR CHAPTER 12

MANUSCRIPT SOURCES

Archives des Petites Sœurs des Pauvres. Testimony of Little Sisters of the Poor: Sœur Thérèse Augustine, Sœur Valentine Joseph. A. Leroy, *Détails complémentaires . . .* op. cit. A. Helleu, *Notes et observations relatives à certains documents faisant partie du dossier de la cause de Jeanne Jugan* (about 1940). *Livre de fondation* of the Saint-Servan house. Legal documents.

Archives de l'Académie française. Mémoire, op. cit.

Archives de l'Oratoire de la Sainte-Face (Tours). Correspondence of M. Dupont.

Archives municipales de Saint-Servan. Mayor's correspondence; Deliberations of the Municipal Council; records of civil registration.

PRINTED SOURCES CONTEMPORARY WITH JEANNE JUGAN

Louis-Napoléon Bonaparte, *Extinction du paupérisme,* Paris, Paguerre, 1844.

L. Veuillot, *Les Petites Sœurs des Pauvres ou le droit à l'assistance selon le christianisme,* in *L'Univers,* 13 September 1848.

LATER STUDIES

J. Delumeau, op. cit.

P. D. Janvier, *Vie de M. Dupont d'après ses écrits et autres documents authentiques,* Tours, Mame, 1879.

C. de La Corbinière, op. cit.

A. Leroy, op. cit.

13

SISTERS OF THE POOR

We have just accompanied Jeanne Jugan, Virginie
Trédaniel, Marie Jamet and Madeleine Bourges as they
served the aged poor from September 1842 to April 1845.
During the same period a more hidden story had been
unfolding in the Maison de la Croix: that of the progressive
development of a religious community. We shall consider
this now.

There was no pre-arranged plan, no sudden break. But
clearly, by this point, the four associates firmly intended to
make their way, if possible, to the religious life properly so
called. Gradually and unhurriedly, they adopted the various elements, from most intimate to most obvious, which
seemed to constitute, to their way of thinking, a life consecrated to God in religion. In their quest for this, they
were to be discreetly and deftly helped by Fr Félix Massot
of the Brothers of St John of God. The almost imperceptible
development was like that of a tiny new leaf, bursting from
the bud and slowly unfolding, tautening its nerves and
eventually spreading wide to the light.

The three youngest of them had already promised obedience to Jeanne (29 May 1842) and taken a vow of chastity
for six months (15 August 1842). On 20 October, Marie
became Jeanne's councillor, taking her place when Jeanne
was away. Together they were to play a special role in the
progressive elaboration of the rule, the points of which, one
by one, were studied either by these two, or by all four,

then put to the practical test, then provisionally fixed. There were to be two inseparable sides to this rule: those points bearing mainly on the personal lives of the Sisters, and those more directly concerned with their functions as hospitallers.

They still kept their everyday regional dress, to wear this out, since they did not have the means to meet the expense of a total change, but the rule stated that 'their clothes are to be of black or brown colour, or at least these colours will predominate; there is to be nothing special or unusual about them.' Like all women of humble condition, they wore a cap, a coif secured by a ribbon under the chin. When they went out, they put on a large cape with a wide round hood, such as we have already described Jeanne Jugan as wearing; it was the cloak in use among the widows of Saint-Servan. Gradually, however, they were to adopt certain usages in common. And for a start, they cut off their hair; thenceforth they wore a head-band under their cap, concealing the forehead.

On 21 November 1842, Jeanne and Marie took a vow of obedience in a private capacity for one year. It was on this occasion, it would seem, that they furnished 'a poor little stable' as an oratory; many years afterwards, when Jeanne was an old woman, she remembered the great joy which she had felt in effecting this transformation.

On 8 December, Virginie and Madeleine took a vow of obedience in their turn. Also, on that day, Marie, Virginie and Madeleine renewed their vow of chastity for one year. Thenceforth, 8 December was to be the day for the renewal of vows, and the Immaculate Virgin would be invoked as patroness of the Association. As physical expression of this taking of vows, the Sisters (like the Brothers of St John of God) were to wear a leather belt and a little crucifix: signs for themselves alone, since not outwardly visible. On this same 8 December, they proceeded to hold a formal election:

that of a Superior. 'The election was held; Jeanne was
elected,' Marie Jamet was to record.

A year went by.

> On 8 December 1843, [Marie went on] the year for which
> Jeanne had been elected Superior being over, a new election
> took place. Jeanne was elected again . . . When her term of
> office as Superior was extended, Jeanne was well known in the
> town; by God's grace, she was so, in a way very advantageous
> to the work for which she had already laboured so hard and
> for which she was to go on labouring zealously and constantly.
> Jeanne, who was the Superior, went on with the collecting,
> Virginie had the clothing, Madeleine the kitchen, and Marie
> (the writer of this) responsibility for the housework and a
> share in the collecting.

This testimony is important and should be noted. To all
appearance, Marie approved the election of her much
admired friend.

But, two weeks later, a disconcerting event was to occur.
Two days before Christmas, the Abbé Le Pailleur called
another meeting of the community and quashed the election which had just taken place. He designated the one
whom he wanted as Superior: this was Marie Jamet. The
four associates bowed to the priest's decision. Long afterwards, on 10 April 1884, hence after Jeanne was dead, the
Abbé Le Pailleur was to recall this 'first Chapter (if I may
call it such) improvised at Saint-Servan, solely on my
inspiration, with my first four poor girls . . . My first spiritual daughter . . . was unanimously elected Superior General at it for, although we only had one house, . . . foresee-
ing what was about to happen, I was anxious to have a
Superior-General there and then.'

We can guess the motives for this curious decision: timid
Marie, aged twenty-three, full of veneration for her spiri-
tual father, was to be a docile instrument in his hands.
Jeanne on the other hand was fifty-one and twenty years

older than he was; she had years of experience behind her; she had been living in Saint-Servan for the previous twenty-six years; many of the people there already held her in the highest admiration. He, too, over the previous five years, had made his mark and might perhaps hope to do much more; the sequence of events certainly suggests it. He was very probably convinced that the four relatively uneducated girls would not be equal to the high demands of their task, since he foresaw how the work was to expand; he himself would have a necessary part in it. But it would have been difficult for him to impose his decisions on Jeanne; with her he would not have a completely free hand.

Be that as it may, he brushed her aside. Long years afterwards, she was to say to him—with a sort of playfulness probably concealing years of suffering—'You have stolen my work from me, but I willingly relinquish it to you!' Hers to know this kind of poverty, too, a much more radical kind than what she had voluntarily embraced: that of giving up to someone else who, she suspected, might not be entirely disinterested, both the final responsibility for the work and the appearance of being its begetter. No word of hers survives from this period, which might allow us to gauge the intensity of her inner conflict. We may suppose that she wondered, before God, 'Have I the right to leave this still-so-fragile work to other hands?' Everything in her attitude gives us to believe that she rose above her anxieties, to commit the future of the work to God who had called it into being, and whose Providence would be well able to take care of it.

In the town, no one knew about this change inside the humble community. When, a year later, the Mayor, Municipal Councillors and parish priest himself addressed a memorial to the French Academy, they were to name Jeanne as the Superior of the community and organiser of the work. 'The persons assisting her', they were to say,

'copy her example.' And what is more, the Abbé Le Pailleur was himself the man who drafted the memorial, with
its potential for attracting substantial funds to the house.
And in Saint-Servan, and soon in other towns, people were
to go on calling the Sisters *the little Jeanne Jugans*. The
unfolding of events will show that for the next ten years,
ten decisive years, Jeanne was to remain the only recognised authority in her expanding work.

But, to return to the Maison de la Croix at the beginning
of 1844: they were beginning to feel worried; no other
associates were joining. A few had thought of doing so; but
the extreme poverty had frightened them off. 'No, my God,
it isn't possible, you can't be demanding that of me!' The
girl who used to pray these words, did in fact become a
Little Sister of the Poor, but much later. Another one used
to pray to St Joseph, wanting to become a religious, 'but
not with the Little Sisters!' She joined, too, in the end.

Marie had a sister a little younger than herself, called
Eulalie (1824–93). For a long while Eulalie felt what
amounted to repulsion for her elder sister's chosen way of
life. She used to say, 'Be off, you and your basket! You
make me feel ashamed . . . Beggar!' But towards the end
of 1843 she came for a few days to replace one of the Sisters
who was ill in bed, and was struck on discovering, from
the inside, how the little community lived, its prayerfulness,
its self-sacrifice; and she decided to join them. She was
received in January 1844. Two other girls made a try, but
did not persevere.

Even so, the community continued to develop its religious form of life. Thus, on 4 February, at the time when,
that year, they were beginning to prepare for Easter, the
Servants of the Poor changed their name and became the
Sisters of the Poor, no doubt the better to express that evangelical brotherliness revealed by Jesus, and their intention
of sharing completely, on an equal footing, with those

brothers and sisters. Each of them also took a name in religion: Jeanne became Sister Marie de la Croix;[1] Marie was Sister Marie Augustine de la Compassion; Virginie, Sister Marie Thérèse de Jésus; and Madeleine, Sister Marie Joseph. Eulalie shortly afterwards was to take the name Sister Marie de la Conception.[2]

Three days later, the four Sisters took private vows of poverty and *hospitality* for one year. In this fourth vow, we note the influence of the Brothers of St John of God, who also practised it. And on 8 December 1844, they renewed the four vows for another year.

During the autumn of 1845, Jeanne went to collect in Dinan. In her heart she always bore, in trusting prayer, a hope for new Sisters, when it should be God's will. It was probably during this stay that she came into contact with a girl called Françoise Trévily (1824–1901). The daughter of a fisherman of Erquy, Françoise also decided to become a Sister of the Poor. At the end of 1845, Jeanne went to fetch her from Erquy, and it is related that, to cross the streams which cut across the beach, fearless and strong, she carried her on her back. Under the name Sister Anne-Marie, Françoise became the sixth *Sister of the Poor*.

SOURCES FOR CHAPTER 13

MANUSCRIPT SOURCES

Archives des Petites Sœurs des Pauvres. Notes of the first Little Sisters of the Poor: Marie Jamet.

---

[1] Known in English-speaking countries as Sister Mary of the Cross.
[2] To avoid confusion, we shall hardly ever use these names in religion, and in any case they came only gradually into use.

Testimony of Little Sisters of the Poor : Sœur Alexis de Sainte Thérèse reported by Sœur Marie-Hortense, Sœur Herminie de Sainte Madeleine, Sœur Ignace de Saint Joseph, Sœur Marie Berchmans, Sœur Marie de Sainte Blandine, Sœur Saint Aurélien, Sœur Thérèse Augustine.

Livre de fondation of the Saint-Servan house. Circular letters of the Abbé Le Pailleur. *Note sur le travail de l'abbé Leroy*, op. cit. A. Leroy, *Détails complémentaires* . . . op. cit.

Archives de l'Académie française. Mémoire, op. cit.

Bibliothèque municipale de Dinan. De L'Hommeau, *Histoire du Vieux Dinan*, vol. III, 1913 (manuscript).

PRINTED SOURCES CONTEMPORARY WITH JEANNE JUGAN

L. Aubineau, op. cit.

L. Odorici, *Recherches sur Dinan et ses environs*, Dinan, Huart, 1857.

Règlement pour la société des Filles du Très-Saint Cœur . . . op. cit.

LATER STUDIES

A. Leroy, op. cit.

14

THE PRIX MONTYON

(1845)

Every year, the French Academy bestowed *Awards for Merit* founded by Monsieur de Montyon to 'reward a poor French man or woman for outstandingly meritorious activity'.

The idea occurred to Jeanne's friends that they might apply for this prize, the amount of which would be very useful. On 21 December 1844, the *Memorial* soliciting it was ready, signed by the parish priest and fourteen municipal councillors, and counter-signed by the Mayor and the Sub-prefect of Saint-Malo. Admittedly, Jeanne had resisted. She pleaded 'with tears that her name should not be mentioned . . . but eventually gave her consent in the interests of her poor.' The *Memorial* itself gives this detail. Note this: what upset Jeanne was that she personally should be put forward; not that the Academy should be approached.

Drawn up and signed by well-informed and disinterested persons, the importance of this text is of the first magnitude; we have already drawn on it several times in earlier chapters. First of all, the authors give an account of the condition of the aged in Saint-Servan.

Although it had a fair-sized population, and a population of seafarers who, all too often decimated by the perils of the sea, left their aged parents without support, Saint-Servan had no hospice or other place to admit the indigent aged of either sex, as a consequence of which many unfortunate old people were exposed to every kind of hardship there. Their sorry state moved Jeanne's heart to compassion; she decided to come to their help.

The text then gives a detailed account of how the first inmates were taken in and how Jeanne was soon to have twelve, then twenty, then thirty and eventually sixty-five old people in her charge. 'How often, herself going to seek them out in their dismal corners, she has persuaded them to go with her or, if they could not walk, has picked them up like a precious burden and cheerfully carried them off to her house!'

Next, the *Memorial* alludes to the children whom Jeanne took in for some time:

> She took in a little girl of five, a crippled orphan called Thérèse Poinso, whom no one wanted; on another occasion, a girl of fourteen, Jeanne Louette, whose unnatural parents had abandoned her on leaving our town; she took this unhappy girl in, as she was being dragged off to a place of prostitution. . . .

Jeanne's true vocation was to look after the aged poor, but it is clear that in the eyes of her fellow-citizens she was the very image of charity to all, and that in any case of hardship which defied solution they had recourse to her. The *Memorial* goes on:

> She is forever on the go, whatever the weather, with a basket over her arm, and this she always brings home full . . .
>
> In pleading (the cause of the poor) she is truly eloquent; she has often been known to burst into tears when explaining their needs. And so it is hard to refuse her, and she has nearly always succeeded in melting even the hardest of hearts . . .
>
> She has truly thrown in her lot with the poor; she dresses like them in what she is given; she lives on left-overs as they do, always making a point of keeping the best bits for those who are sick or more infirm; and the persons assisting her copy her example . . .

Lastly, order reigns in this house. The work is organised there. . . . The poor are treated kindly and kept very clean.

We shall have more to say about this invaluable testimony. What is of interest to us here is that it was well received by those to whom it was addressed. Less than a year later, the Mayor of Saint-Servan was informed that a First Prize worth three thousand francs had been awarded by the Academy to *Miss Jeanne Jugan*. As we have seen, this sum arrived at just the right moment to pay for the roof and furnishing of the new building added to the house.

The newspapers reported how on 11 December 1845 at the annual meeting of the Academy, Monsieur André Dupin had delivered the customary discourse. Under the cupola, before a distinguished audience, among whom could be seen Messrs de Chateaubriand, de Lamartine, Hugo, Thiers, Guizot and Sainte-Beuve, Monsieur Dupin, Senior, a Voltairean if ever there was one, had delivered the eulogy on humble Jeanne Jugan. In the days following, the *Journal des Débats*, the *Correspondant*, the *Illustration* and many local papers in Brittany carried this news item or reprinted Dupin's speech.

Jeanne would probably have known nothing about all this if she had not been sent several copies of the text about herself. She realised that she could make use of the *Academy Pamphlet*, as she called it, to recommend her work to the civil authorities in the towns where she proposed to go collecting.

We should not omit to mention that as a spin-off from the Montyon Award she also received the unexpected homage of a Masonic lodge: a gold medal awarded to this 'admirable girl', said the address. Jeanne accepted it, had it melted down, and the gold became the bowl of a chalice for the chapel.

It is very impressive to observe how instinctively Jeanne considered it perfectly normal for the most profane organi-

sations of this world, far removed from the familiar con-
fines of the Church, to recognise her solidarity with the
poor and associate themselves with this.

In this same spirit, we shall see her confidently
approaching the civil and military authorities in the towns
which she was later to visit. After Rennes, it would be
Dinan, then Tours, Angers, Chartres, Brest and many
other cities.

On 19 January, she did indeed set out for Rennes. Fear-
lessly or conquering her fear, she was going to collect for
the poor of Saint-Servan, now too numerous for their fellow-citizens to be able to support them. The people of
Saint-Servan for their part wanted Jeanne to go to Rennes.
Flattered by the fame of their collecting-sister, now one of
the glories of their country, they wanted to use her on
behalf of their hospice. She therefore set out, armed with
a letter of recommendation from the Mayor of Saint-Servan
and with the Academy discourse. A certain fame, inspired
by the said discourse, doubtless preceded her.

Thus, leaving port and coastal fishing, she headed out
to sea, like her father, her brother and so many other sailors
of Cancale. Her particular sea was to be the highways and
byways of the period, with their own particular hardships
and dangers. And city life too, of which she had no experience hitherto.

SOURCES FOR CHAPTER 14

MANUSCRIPT SOURCES

Archives des Petites Sœurs des Pauvres. A. Helleu, *Notes et obser-
vations* . . . op. cit.
Livre de fondation of the Saint-Servan house.
Archives de l'Académie française. Mémoire, op. cit.

PRINTED SOURCES CONTEMPORARY WITH JEANNE JUGAN

A. Dupin, *Discours* delivered 11 December 1845. *Le Journal des débats*, 12 December 1845. *Le Journal de Rennes*, 13 December 1845. *Le Correspondant*, 15 December 1845. *La Vigie de l'Ouest*, 16 December 1845. *L'Auxiliaire Breton*, 16 December 1845. *Le Progrès, Courrier de Bretagne*, 17 December 1845. *Le Messager Breton*, 18 December 1845; 25 December 1845. *L'Impartial de Bretagne*, 19 December 1845. Revue *L'Illustration*, 20 December 1845. Le *Publicateur des Côtes-du-Nord*, 27 December 1845. Le *Musée des familles*, 27 December 1845. Y. Tennaëc (= A. Chevremont), *La destinée du Pauvre*, Rennes, Marteville, 1846; *Clairières*, Rennes, Marteville, 1848 and Paris, Paul Servan, 1873.

LATER STUDIES

A. Leroy, op. cit.

15

COLLECTING AT RENNES

(1846)

At Rennes, Jeanne seems to have taken her unfamiliar surroundings in her stride. She lodged with a tradeswoman called Mademoiselle Morel, who had helped with the Saint-Servan home in its early days. On her arrival, she called on the Bishop, and next on a Monsieur Chevremont who was Secretary-General of the Prefecture and whom she knew to be well disposed. He in turn introduced her to the Prefect. The latter gave her written authorisation to collect in the Department.

Next and without hesitation, she contacted the Press, which had already been writing about her a month earlier. Helped by her benefactors, she had a notice printed about her collection. The *Auxiliaire Breton* published it on 22 January; the *Journal de Rennes*, on 24 January. Here is an extract from the article appearing in the *Auxiliaire Breton*.

Poor Jeanne! She is the image of charity on earth! Yesterday she told us about a great stroke of luck which she had had. A little while ago, she had taken three new invalids into her house. One of them had only a filthy hole to live in; the other had not slept in a bed for twenty years! Jeanne and two of her assistants had to turn out to make room for the newcomers. 'Jeanne, but where did you sleep?' 'On the floor, of course!' 'But wasn't it very hard?' 'We never noticed. We were so happy to think that our three poor people were happy, in comfortable beds!'

In these articles, she suggested that people who were willing to send an offering should give their address to the newspaper office. As a result, they would not only be brought individually into contact with Jeanne but also into contact with one another, and the network of collaborators already sketchily existing at Rennes would thus expand and acquire a bit of body. Jeanne had a kind of innate sense of human solidarity. Wherever she passed, she contributed either to bringing it to birth or to making it grow.

Forthwith, she informed her Superior, Marie Jamet, about her activities. This letter has disappeared, like all her other writings, but we have the young Superior's answer.[1] From it we learn that from the first moments of Jeanne's stay in Rennes, she had been concerned about the condition of the poor there. She had seen them begging in the streets, people had talked to her about them. She had sensed the extent of the poverty, the urgent desire for relief, and her letter had given a 'picture' of this. And already she was outlining a plan for a house to be opened in Rennes . . . Marie Jamet counselled her to prudence.

In default of Jeanne's own *picture*, here is another one, probably less colourful, drawn five years later by a certain Théodore Letestu, Principal Secretary to the Mayor's Office, who was much concerned for the poor and who played a notable part in establishing the Little Sisters of the Poor in Rennes.

> There is not a soul among us whose heart is not wrung by the at once saddening and shaming spectacle which beggary presents to our eyes! No one who, seeing these beggars, be they children or old people, infirm or healthy, wandering through our streets and public places, asking for alms, has not many a time expressed the wish that an end could be put to such a state of affairs.

[1] For the text of the letter, see end of chapter.

Efforts had indeed been made. First of all, at the 'General Hospice' in Rennes there was a section for the 'aged and infirm' (those who were bed-ridden) consisting of about five hundred beds—all full—but in the very mediocre conditions typical of hospitals of the period. There were also various private concerns, soup-kitchens for the indigent, various services organised by the clergy, and a Charity Office (official after 1821) which distributed help and medication. On a number of occasions, particularly in 1842, charitable people had got together to collect funds with a view to opening the hostels needed, but nothing had come of all this before Jeanne's arrival.

In point of fact there were fewer beggars, proportionally, than there were at Saint-Servan: in 1840, out of a population of about thirty thousand inhabitants, there were reckoned to be three hundred and two (not counting more than a hundred intruders, not domiciled in Rennes); in 1852, after the opening of the home, there were still 233 of them.

Nonetheless, there was a great deal of hardship in the working-class quarters of the town: the families there knew the trials of unemployment, with no defence against illness, living on little, from hand to mouth, virtually without any security (despite the creation in 1830 of a Provident Savings Bank, which was a non-profit-making and very active charitable institution). In January 1847, a year after Jeanne's arrival, rioting broke out in these quarters, an explosion of wrath at the bakers' decision not to give away Epiphany buns that year: pillaging of grain-ships, attack on a bakery, skirmishes with the police. Mgr Brossais Saint-Marc, whose baker had sent him some buns, returned them with the words, 'As long as there are so many wretched people without bread, I do not wish my household to eat cakes!' The municipality was responsible for these poor people. Every year it set aside certain funds

The towers of the Porte de Brest in the fortifications of Dinan. Jeanne set up house in these temporary quarters in August 1846 (see Chapter 17)

Formerly a spinning factory, La Piletière on the outskirts of Rennes became a home for the aged in 1852. Jeanne lived there for four years (see Chapter 21)

Scene from hospitaller life in London, by James Collinson (for explanation, see Appendix IV)—*Photo Jean Fortier*

Nous, Préfet de Maine & Loire

Vu les renseignements qui nous ont été fournis sur les nombreux services rendus aux pauvres par la Dame Jeanne Jugan et sur le désintéressement dont elle n'a cessé de faire preuve, ainsi que les petites sœurs;

Autorisons cette Dame à effectuer dans toute l'étendue du département de Maine & Loire, une ou plusieurs quêtes en faveur de l'œuvre qu'elle a fondé et invitons les autorités civiles et militaires à lui accorder, au besoin, protection pour l'accomplissement de sa mission charitable.

Accordons la même autorisation aux petites sœurs des pauvres qui l'aident dans ses bonnes œuvres.

En Préfecture, à Angers, le 26 Juin 18..

Le Préfet,

Creases in the parchment, and finger-marks on this collecting-permit, prove how Jeanne walked the roads of Anjou (see Chapter 20) to finance 'charitable work', 'an act of benevolence towards the indigent working-class'.

It was in this town, where goodwill was not lacking, though helpless when faced with so much hardship, that Jeanne carried on with her collecting.

This was not always easy. We see her, for instance, in a government office (admittedly less impersonal than today). The woman behind the desk (or was it the civil servant's wife?) tries to dissuade her, 'It's an act of madness,' she says. 'Quite so, my dear good lady, an act of madness, you might say an impossibility! But if God is for us, it will come about.' 'But, my dear Jeanne, the officials at top level have refused out of hand!' 'Couldn't I just have a word with them? Do help me, please!' 'Mr C — will be here in an hour, if you have the courage . . .' 'Oh, dear kind lady, I'm not short on courage . . . Do let me wait.' 'Very well, Jeanne, just as you please!'

At this point she retires into a corner, takes an old prayerbook in a battered cloth cover out of her pocket and makes herself alone with God. When the important personage appears, she goes straight up to him, gives him such simple reasons, speaks to him so sweetly and trustingly, so respectfully too, that she gets what the poor are waiting for. *If God is for us, it will come about.*

One day when she was out collecting, a rich, hard-hearted man started hectoring her; beside himself, he even pushed her away from him, sending her tumbling down the stairs, from step to step, all the way from second to first-floor landing. Alarmed at the fall, 'Have I hurt you, Sister?' 'A bit, sir.' 'No, have you really hurt yourself?' 'Oh, think nothing of it, kind sir.' 'But can you walk? Is anything broken?' 'Oh, I can walk all right, kind sir, I can make my own way down.' 'No, Sister, come back up here, come back, take this!' And he handed her a hundred francs.

Jeanne was received at table by 'influential ladies':

Madame Barbedor, a grocer's wife; Mme de La Grasserie, who ten years later was to have Jeanne's portrait painted; Mme de Montigny, who became a Little Sister; there was also Monsieur Vatar, who was related to the Bishop; and a doctor called Monsieur Tual.

When she went to see the Bishop, she had been very kindly received. Mgr Brossais Saint-Marc had given her his personal contribution and added maliciously, 'I'm afraid you are going to wrong the poor of Rennes!' Jeanne replied in all seriousness, 'I ask nothing better than to take nothing back to Saint-Servan and to look after the poor people of Rennes!'

In point of fact, the abundant results of her collecting were certainly to be devoted to the poor of Saint-Servan: their fellow-citizens would not have allowed it to be other-wise! But Jeanne was forthwith to put herself at the service of those who needed her in Rennes. Far from despoiling Rennes to clothe Saint-Servan, she conferred wealth on Rennes by laying the foundations of organised charity there and by stimulating the awareness of collective responsibil-ity for the more deprived members of society.

LETTER OF MARIE JAMET

Saint-Servan, 26 January 1846

My dear child,
How often I blessed Divine Providence while reading your letter! How good God is to allow a poor girl like you to be so well received! It has given me great pleasure to see the handsome way in which you have been treated by the kind lady who has been so good as to offer you hospitality. Please convey our deep gratitude to her and tell her that we pray for God's blessing on her. All the same, my child, take care not to be obtrusive and,

however little of a nuisance you may be, do not take advantage of this excellent person's kindness.

With similar joy, I have read about your favourable reception by the Prefect, the Bishop's blessing, the help that Monsieur Chevremont is giving you and how you have been well received everywhere, to the point where influential ladies do you the honour of admitting you to their table. Even so, my child, I recommend you to show how grateful you are and to behave in all circumstances with great politeness and restraint. I also recommend you to beware of conceiving the least feeling of self-esteem. Be very sure that, if people treat you like this, they do it not because of you but because God allows it for the greater good of his poor. As far as you yourself are concerned, always consider yourself what you truly are, that is to say, poor, weak, wretched and incapable of all good.

My child, I also praise you for your proper sentiments as regards the poor of Rennes. From the picture you have given me, it seems that they are sadly neglected. My heart is torn, like yours. Undoubtedly it would be a very fine thing, as you say, if they had a house like ours. My child, your desires are excellent but the matter is not simple. If all that was needed were devoted children, we could indeed offer some, but, as you must know, a thing of this sort cannot be set up without the consent of the Prefect and probably of the Mayor, or without the approval of many other people: which is no easy matter. It is only easy and possible to God. My child, once again I recommend you humility, restraint, discretion and prudence. We pray God and his holy Mother that these graces may be granted you. Go on with your collecting but do not be too insistent. Your companions are well. The *good dear Father* is well and prays for you. Do not forget him in your prayers. For myself, I am now better and have resumed my normal duties. Would you please send us, through the good offices of Mlle Morel as before, a letter to reach us next Sunday or Saturday, giving us further news if you have any. Monsieur Diot, curate of Saint-Servan, will be passing through Rennes next week and will bring you the answer. We shall let you know, if we can, the date and time so that he can see you.

Once again, would you please convey my deep gratitude to Mlle Morel.

I kiss you very tenderly, dear child, and am in Our Lord, at the feet of Mary,

Your Mother

Marie Jamet

The Abbé Le Pailleur's influence is apparent in this letter; it is hard to imagine Marie Jamet unprompted using such a condescending tone when addressing Jeanne.

SOURCES FOR CHAPTER 15

MANUSCRIPT SOURCES

Archives des Petites Sœurs des Pauvres. Letters of the first Little Sisters of the Poor : Marie Jamet. *Livre de fondation* of the Rennes house. Letter of Fr Lelièvre, 25 June 1874.

A. Leroy, *Détails complémentaires . . .* op. cit.

Archives municipales de Rennes. Comptes de gestion des hospices civils de Rennes, Q 14/2.

Archives de l'Oratoire de la Sainte-Face (Tours). Correspondence of M. Dupont.

PRINTED SOURCES CONTEMPORARY WITH JEANNE JUGAN

Extrait du rapport du maire sur le budget supplémentaire de 1842, etc. printed, 1843, Arch. mun. de Rennes, C/2 12.

T. Letestu, *Mémoire sur l'extinction de la mendicité dans la ville de Rennes, etc.,* printed, 1854, Arch. mun. de Rennes, C/7 7. *L'Auxiliaire Breton,* 22 January; 3 and 31 March; 11 April 1846. *Le Journal de Rennes,* 26 January 1846. *Le Messager breton,* 16 April 1846. *Le Dinannais,* 8 March and 19 April 1846. *Le Publicateur des Côtes-du-Nord,* 14 March 1846. *L'Impartial, journal de Bretagne,* 6 March 1846.

LATER STUDIES

H. Joüin, *Rennes il y a cent ans,* series I, II, III, Rennes, Imprimerie bretonne, 1933.

C. de La Corbinière, op. cit.

A. Leroy, op. cit.

J. Meyer, *Histoire de Rennes,* Paris, Privat, 1972.

J. Vidalenc, op. cit.

16

THE FOUNDATION AT RENNES

(1846)

Jeanne had arrived in Rennes on 19 January, intending to collect for Saint-Servan. Marie Jamet's reply, dated 26 January, makes it clear that Jeanne had already informed her of the need for a foundation in that town. On 14 February we learn—again through Marie Jamet—that Jeanne was simultaneously collecting for Saint-Servan and making preparations for a new foundation. Kindly received by Mgr Brossais Saint-Marc, she had already obtained authorisation from the Prefect and the Mayor.

On 28 February, Marie Jamet joined her to begin the new house. Jeanne had already rented a large room with a little room attached to it; there they set up house with a poor infirm blind woman, as at Saint-Servan. Soon there were ten inmates, who were very happy with Miss Marie and Miss Jeanne, as they called them.

They had found a friendly and resourceful helper in the person of Monsieur Varangot, the manager of the optic telegraph at Rennes; this method of communication, established in 1832 as we have said, was only any good in clear weather—so it was probably hardly used at all. And the manager had plenty of free time, which he filled by making furniture as a hobby. He had known the Sisters at Saint-Servan and now paid them a visit. Seeing them poorly equipped, he made them a bed. A little later, he came again; again they were sleeping on the floor, having given up their bed to an old woman. He made them another, insisting that they should use it themselves.

On 3 March, the *Auxiliaire Breton* printed a new announcement from Jeanne. In it she published the results of her collecting over the previous month. One thousand, eight hundred francs[1] and a quantity of clothes and furniture. This was to be used for the home at Rennes. On 14 March, the article was reprinted in the *Publicateur des Côtes-du-Nord*, at Saint-Brieuc, and by some papers in Dinan; there, too, there was interest in Jeanne.

But the premises were too small. The two Sisters went looking for a house. They made a prayerful search. The search proving vain, they urgently confided their problem to St Joseph (who was to take an increasingly important place in the prayers of the Little Sisters of the Poor). On 19 March, his feast-day, Marie Jamet was praying in the church of All Saints;[2] possibly she was reminding the Lord's foster father of the cowshed at Bethlehem and the house at Nazareth. Someone came up to her and said, 'Have you got a house?' 'Not yet.' 'I've just the thing for you.' They went and looked. The house, lying in the suburbs of La Madeleine, in the same parish, could accommodate forty or fifty poor people, and a dependent building would serve as chapel. With the agreement of Saint-Servan, the contract was signed on 25 March. They moved in the same day; some soldiers helped with the house-moving and with transporting the old women.

[1] The figure should be multiplied by fifteen or twenty to give the modern equivalent.

[2] In his work, *L'Église de Toussaints* (All Saints' Church), Rennes, Simon Press, 1973, Monsieur F. Bergot, Curator of the Museum of Fine Arts, Rennes, Curator of Antiquities and Fine Arts for Ille-et-Vilaine, writes,

At no moment in our study have we considered this building as lacking a soul, even less as distinct from those souls whose spiritual experiences in it remain known to themselves alone. Let one only, the humblest, undoubtedly one of the most charitable, be recalled, that 'great-hearted maid' called Jeanne Jugan, at prayer among her poor, at the far end of one of the aisles of her parish church.

Others arrived. And the *Auxiliaire Breton* of 31 March stated that Jeanne, 'thanks to the tireless collecting in which she has been engaged, has gathered enough furniture already to be able to admit sixteen poor people.' On 11 April, the same papers published the text of an extremely kindly-worded authorisation granted by the Mayor, allowing Jeanne to go on collecting in Rennes. In it, we read, 'The hospice is by way of prospering . . . Jeanne Jugan is pursuing her charitable mission with unabated zeal. . . . She devotes herself to it with complete abnegation and untiring energy . . . having no other resources . . . than her trust in Providence.' Two Dinan papers, on 16 and 19 April, were to reprint this.

At about this time, they took in two beggar-women whom people had long been accustomed to see kneeling on the steps of a church. 'Kind souls knew them as Faith and Hope, and the better informed as the two toss-pots.' They had put up a long resistance, but eventually entered the hospice. In a little while they were reformed characters. There was also the all-too-famous Jeanne Dada, whose behaviour was common knowledge throughout Rennes. She went to live with the Sisters; soon she was another woman!

To feed and look after all these people needed staff. Jeanne was out collecting, and the young *Superior-General* could not do all the work on her own. In April, four young Sisters arrived from Saint-Servan; among them was Françoise Trévily, whom Jeanne forthwith initiated into collecting. A Rennes girl offered herself as a postulant—Jeanne-Marie Buis, maid to Mlle Morel with whom Jeanne had lodged on arriving in Rennes. Jeanne had made a conquest of her and she now came to put herself at the service of the poor. On 9 May, youthful Eulalie Jamet was appointed Superior of the new community. Her sister, now released, went back to Saint-Servan, taking two postulants from Rennes with her; she was to find others at Saint-Servan.

Life was tough at the new home. To economise, they baked the bread at home. Sometimes, to be of service to their benefactors, they would act as nurses, spending the night with them, between two days of collecting. And collecting itself was tiring: they had no donkey, they had to carry everything themselves. Young Françoise Trévily put these details on record, adding that, 'sometimes, when she put her bowls down, she couldn't tell if she had any shoulders left.' 'We are so tired,' Eulalie wrote for her part, 'that we haven't the energy left to pray to God.'

People got used to seeing the Little Sisters passing in their poor clothes. Eulalie, who in former days had blamed her sister for being so shabbily dressed, now made fun of herself. 'I was rather tubby,' she was to relate, 'and with my two baskets, at Rennes as at Saint-Servan, I took up the whole street. What with my coarse old skirts and patched up shoes, everyone used to laugh. . . . We offer all this to God for some old person's conversion, and our hearts rejoice!'

And in fact the little community had every reason to be joyful; they often had direct experience of God's marvellous generosity in response to their trust. One day, Eulalie relates,

> we were getting ready to do the washing. No wood. I went to the wood-pile but there were only a few big logs left and no one to cut them up. We resorted to prayer, since it was absolutely essential for the linen to be washed. Soon afterwards, along came a cart full of wood. The carter told us that his master had come into the yard and said, 'Make up a cart-load of wood for the Little Sisters,' and as he was getting ready to load up the wood, the master came back and said, 'The Sisters are so poor that they won't be able to pay anyone to chop it up for them; take it ready chopped.'

One evening, [her account goes on] the Kitchen-Sister came and asked if she should ring for supper as she had nothing to give the Sisters. 'Have the poor eaten all they want?' I asked. 'Yes, Mother.' 'That's all right,' I said. 'You have warned me too late, it's suppertime already, but ring the bell all the same to observe the rule!' We went into the refectory. After grace, the reading began [note in the passage these forms of *regular* life already in use], then someone rang the doorbell. Somebody's servant had arrived, loaded down, bringing a complete supper; nothing was missing. The Sister came back overcome and trembling at the way Divine Providence had been so prompt to help us.

These *fioretti* provide a perfect illustration of the insanely confident atmosphere of faith in which the Sisters lived. They were true sisters of Jeanne Jugan and sisters of the poor.

Was Jeanne herself present at the events which we have just reported? Possibly; for she was at the Rennes house during this period. Or possibly she was away collecting, for she was sent out of Rennes on a number of occasions. In May, for example, Eulalie wrote to her sister and Superior, 'Sister Jeanne has been collecting at Vitré and Fougères and has had a good reception everywhere. At Fougères, she was given 325 francs; at Vitré, 238 francs. . . . I have had a letter from Vitré: two young persons are offering themselves as postulants; one of them is 37 years old and the other 28—rather old.' (Remember that the Superior at Rennes was 22 and the Superior-General, 26!) We may reasonably infer a connection between Jeanne's visit to Vitré and the two candidates' application; it was often like this. Without words, she would say, 'Come, follow me!' At the beginning of July, it was Marie's turn to write from Saint-Servan, telling her sister, 'Send Jeanne to the parishes nearest to Rennes.' And she adds—an amusing detail—'She is not to have her picture painted!' Had they got wind of some scheme on the part of her admirers?

It was perhaps about now that Jeanne got as far as Redon. She rang the doorbell of the Eudist college (she was somewhat of a Eudist herself). One of the Fathers related,

> I went to see her in the parlour and she electrified me. . . .
> Without more ado, I took her into our senior boarders' study-room. There were about a hundred of them in it . . . and Jeanne in simple and direct terms explained the object of her mission. Amazed and deeply moved, all those pupils emptied out everything in their pockets and desks.

Pupils and teachers alike were long to remember the visit.

During this spring at Rennes, Monsieur Dupont of Tours wrote to the Abbé Le Pailleur, 'Everything you tell me overwhelms me with joy but makes me also very anxious to see our poor people here too find mothers, bread, a cot, attention, prayers. All these they utterly lack. Tell Jeanne this quietly, tactfully, for fear it should break her heart!' How well he understood her! She was to go to Tours, but the time had not yet come.

In Rennes for the time being, clouds were to darken the horizon. And Monsieur Le Pailleur was not uninvolved in this. Ever a man of new ideas, he had conceived the scheme of founding a sort of missionary community with two of his colleagues at Saint-Servan to evangelise the least Christian parts of France. And Monsieur Dupont, in point of fact, having inherited a property in Seine-et-Marne, had put it at their disposal. The next thing was to get permission from Mgr Brossais Saint-Marc, but this did not come. Apparently, the three young priests, forcing their Bishop's hand, went off to Bougligny without written authorisation. They were to stay there for three years.

The Bishop was much displeased at this and his displeasure recoiled on the Little Sisters. He found out that

they had not applied for permission to establish themselves
in Rennes: it was a clandestine foundation! And he laid the
blame on the Abbé Gandon, curate of the parish of All
Saints, whom Jeanne had chosen as her confessor on arriving at Rennes and who now stood up for them. True, they
had never made an official application, but everything had
been done with the knowledge and approval of the Bishop,
who knew the Sisters well. The parish priest of All Saints,
Monsieur Berthelot, who valued their work, went to see
the Bishop: the storm was a severe one! The Sisters, Mgr
Brossais Saint-Marc insisted, were to close their home and
go back to Saint-Servan; otherwise, they would be deprived
of the sacraments. The Abbé Gandon advised them to take
action themselves. Apparently Jeanne and Eulalie, very
little and very humble, went to see the Bishop themselves.
'My lord,' said Jeanne, 'we are such little, such weak, girls,
that it never entered our heads that we should need your
permission to work for the good of the poor. But since we
have so displeased your Greatness, we shall leave and put
our old folk back in the street again. How unhappy they
will be!' 'Oh, you will, will you? So that I shall be stoned
in your part of the town and told that I'm responsible for
making you leave? No! You stay!' 'But, my Lord, we are
religious . . . How can we stay here without going to confes-
sion and approaching the Holy Table?' 'What about that
Abbé Gandon, who's caused all this trouble? Tell him to
confess you!'

'We are religious,' they said. Actually, they were not
that, quite yet, not having received any official approval as
a community. But they seriously desired to be so and were
preparing themselves for this. On 1 May of this same year
1846, probably with the help of Fr Félix Massot of St John
of God, they had drawn up a more elaborate rule. It is
worth spending a little while studying this document. In
it, various sources of inspiration may be detected.

Clearly the spirit of St John Eudes, mediated through Jeanne, was still, as it were, the breath quickening the little group. Discreet but sure, we again see the influence of the Third Order of the Heart of Mary. The frequent recitation of the *Monstra te esse matrem* and above all the noon devotions—litany of the Holy Name of Jesus and individual examination of conscience—are derived from this.

The contribution of the Brothers of St John of God becomes even more evident. Like them, the Sisters decide to base themselves on one of the great traditions of the Church: the Rule of St Augustine. More particularly, they adopt certain points characteristic of the Brothers' Constitutions: several passages concerning hospitaller usages have been copied word for word, the only difference being that the 1717 translation still used by the French Brothers has been modernised. We quote a few striking parallels:

CONSTITUTIONS OF THE BROTHERS OF SAINT JOHN OF GOD (1717)	RULE OF THE SISTERS OF THE POOR (1846)
Chap. VIII. . . . On coming out of morning prayer, they *will go to the infirmaries*, where they will visit the sick poor *and do what they can to comfort and cheer them, will make their beds and perform such other charitable acts as need requires.*	Chap. VII. . . . In the morning, the Sisters of the Poor *will go to the rooms of the* infirm or sick *aged poor and do what they can to comfort and cheer them.* . . . They *will make their beds and perform other charitable acts for them as need requires.*
Chap. XVI. The duty of opening and closing the Convent door must be	Chap. XXIII. This job (of porteress) being extremely important, . . . it will be

entrusted to a religious *of mature years* and good example ... *who will not annoy people with too many questions and not vex them by indiscreet words;* who knows how to calm those who take offence, and *to edify by word or example* all those who stay with him or *who have dealings with him. He will always keep the door closed.*

entrusted to a sister *of mature years* and great regularity, who will be kind and gentle to the aged poor, on no account arguing with them ... *not annoying or vexing anyone with too many questions or by indiscreet words,* but knowing how to behave and answer prudently, in a word, *edifying by word and example* the persons *who have dealings with her. She will always keep the door closed.* ...

Chap. XXXI. (The Subprior) *will assist the Prior in all loyalty, will always procure peace between him and the Convent, without showing favour for those who trouble the repose of others, or for the disobedient; and he will always intercede with the Prior* on matters lawful and right.

Chap. XVI. ... The Sister Councillor *will loyally assist the Mother Superior ... she will procure peace between the Mother Superior and the Sisters, without* ever *showing favour for those who trouble the repose of others, or for the disobedient. She will intercede with the Mother Superior* on behalf of those who are penitent.

Chap. XXXIV. (The First Infirmarian) ... He *will take great care* ... *that the Infirmaries are clean and scented* ... *that the sick are kept clean, often changing their night-shirts and sheets* ... *In his care he*

Chap. XX. (The Sister Infirmarian) *will take care that the infirmaries are clean and scented* ... *and that the sick are kept clean, often changing their nightshirts and sheets* ... *In her care, she will have the jams,*

will have the jams and refresh-	potions *and* other *refreshments*
ments, and he will distribute	*. . . and she will distribute these*
some of these daily to the	to each according to need.
sick poor.	

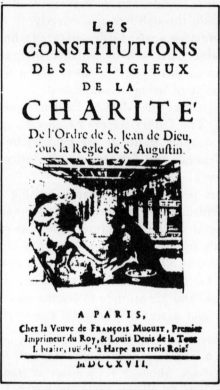

Title page of the Constitutions of the Brothers of St John of God
(see Chapters 16 and 21).

Sometimes the resemblance is less literal, but the spirit remains the same. Did Jeanne take a personal part in drafting this? We do not know, but a formula such as the following, which has no equivalent in the Rule of the Brothers of St John of God, may well bear her stamp: 'Prayer, which is needful to all, (is) even more needful to the children of this poor family who rely on God alone' (Chap. I).

Be that as it may, we may suppose that this rule delighted her: in it, she would have seen an advance in the search for God's purpose, and she would have borne it in her suppliant, wonder-struck prayers. God had already done so much, through her own poverty, in the course of the seven previous years! Little she cared whether she had a recognisable part in it or whether she vanished completely from earthly eyes. She knew that a work of grace was in process of being accomplished.

In this 1846 text, the Abbé Le Pailleur's presence is also to be seen: 'The Father Superior-General', it states, 'will enjoy all the same rights as are enjoyed by the Mother Superior-General, and furthermore the latter will submit to and obey him in all things.'

From this period a somewhat surprising letter of his survives, addressed to Monsieur Chevremont, the Secretary-General of the Prefecture, who had given Jeanne such a kindly reception in January. Written after the initial successes of the collections, the letter both reveals the role which M. Le Pailleur ascribed to himself in the Little Sisters' work, and his attitude to Jeanne—a cross between admiration and a sort of disdainful commiseration:

> I do not know, sir, how to express our gratitude to you for all you have done for our poor Jeanne. It is truly in the order of the miraculous. Although I am aware of Jeanne's devotion and of her love for all who suffer and grieve, I was far from expecting such complete success. After God, the Disposer of hearts, I attribute it to the kind protector whom she has been so fortunate as to find in you.

This letter was in no way to diminish the high esteem in which Monsieur Chevremont held Jeanne. We have proof of this in a little collection of poems entitled *The Fate of the Poor, verses dedicated to Jeanne Jugan* and preceded by a *Letter to Monsieur de Chateaubriand*, which appeared in Rennes in

June 1846 under the pen-name Yves Tennaëc (Marteville, limited edition). The introduction describes Jeanne as she was known in Rennes. She exerts a seductive influence, 'everybody wants to see her'; she is well received everywhere. The author evokes 'her sad, sweet face, her cheeks grown pale by night-watching, her eyes normally so calm but on occasion so radiant'. He next describes her work, her forty old women brought back to life 'under the maternal care of Jeanne and three of her companions summoned by her once again to take their place beside her . . . This I have seen for myself.' It is clear that he is eloquently aware both of her quality of character and of her actual function in the growing community. As regards the verses, unfortunately their poetic value in no way equals M. Chevremont's professed enthusiasm for Jeanne,[3] but in him she had a true friend.

She had many others in Rennes as well. A few years later, just at the time when, in this same town, Jeanne was to find herself condemned to final retirement, Monsieur Letestu (whom we have already met) was to pay homage before the Municipal Council to the association of the Little Sisters of the Poor, 'personified in our town by the name of a modest woman, Jeanne Jugan, the first of her companions to come among us and exercise her humble and devout ministry here'.

For Jeanne and her sisters, when all is said and done, the first months spent in Rennes had been a great adventure in faith. In a letter dated 17 July, Marie Jamet expressed her amazement at God's work, 'Since the house at Rennes began, what numberless graces he has granted us!'

[3] This booklet later formed a chapter in a collection which came out in 1848 called *Clairières* (Rennes, Marteville). The volume was reprinted in 1873 (Paris, Paul Servan). In this, the introduction about Jeanne Jugan was expanded by two paragraphs laying stress on her role as foundress, 'More than two hundred houses, founded in France and in the rest of Europe, attest the fruitfulness of her original idea and the rapid development of her undertaking.'

SOURCES FOR CHAPTER 16

MANUSCRIPT SOURCES

Archives des Petites Sœurs des Pauvres. Letters and fragments of the first Little Sisters of the Poor : Marie Jamet, Eulalie Jamet.

Testimony of Little Sisters of the Poor : Françoise Trévily and Eulalie Jamet reported by A. Leroy. Letter of Mme Varangot.

Livre de fondation of the Rennes house; *Règlement* of 1 May 1846. Photocopy of an article on M. Chevremont. A. Leroy, *Détails complémentaires* . . . op. cit.

Archives de l'Oratoire de la Sainte-Face (Tours). Correspondence of M. Dupont.

PRINTED SOURCES CONTEMPORARY WITH JEANNE JUGAN

Newspaper articles : references have been grouped together at the end of Chapter 15.

L. Aubineau, op. cit.

T. Letestu, *Rapport sur l'extinction de la mendicité*, op. cit.

Y. Tennaëc (= A. Chevremont), *La destinée du pauvre*, op. cit.

Les constitutions des religieux de la Charité de l'Ordre de Saint-Jean-de-Dieu sous la Règle de Saint-Augustin, Paris, 1717.

Règlement des Sœurs des Pauvres (1846).

Règlement pour la société des Filles du Très-Saint Cœur . . ., op. cit.

LATER STUDIES

C. de La Corbinière, op. cit.

A. Leroy, op. cit.

P. Tiriaux, *Notice biographique sur M. l'abbé Gandon*, by one of his curates, Rennes, Simon, 1896.

17

DINAN

(1846)

While Jeanne was collecting in Rennes and its environs, the decision had been reached at Saint-Servan to lay the foundations for a third house. A tradeswoman of Dinan, Mademoiselle Follen, who had helped with the foundation at Saint-Servan, wanted to see a similar house opened in her own town.

Marie had been to collect there as early as June 1846. The result had not been negligible but many people were holding back; they wanted Jeanne Jugan, she was the one they would give to. 'I have been to a number of middle-class people,' Marie notes, 'and they told me that they will give. One lady promised me a hundred francs but actually gave me twenty-five. The others ask for Jeanne and say that they will give to her.' Father Claude-Marie Gandet himself, the then Prior of the Brothers of St John of God at Dinan, insisted that Jeanne should be sent to make the foundation.

The local newspapers had already written about her when she received the Montyon Award and had later printed reports about her activities in the town of Rennes. On 25 June, the *Messager Breton* reported, 'A virtuous priest is said to be going to set up a home for the aged. The house, modelled on those founded by Jeanne Jugan, will it is hoped contain about a hundred beds.' As far as public opinion was concerned, Jeanne Jugan was still very much the foundress and she it was who had the public's confidence.

But she would need considerable tact to establish herself within an already existing charitable network, of which the people of Dinan seem to have been justly proud. The new home would have to take its place alongside several 'charitable institutions powerfully geared to doing good': the civil hospice for the aged and infirm, the refuge for poor children, the work of the Daughters of Wisdom, welfare offices—all this financially supported by the town. Shortly after Jeanne's arrival, a man of standing, a retired major, was to write with soldierly forcefulness in *Le Dinannais*,

> Jeanne Jugan has just been given permission to set up a new Home for the indigent aged. Without going into the question here as to whether this new establishment is needed in Dinan, I think it would be only reasonable to incorporate it into the local welfare organisation, so that it can operate in conjunction with the others, all under the supervision of the Central Welfare Office.

A word to the wise is enough! We may add that this gentleman, as well as a number of leading citizens of Dinan, belonged to a 'society for the suppression of begging', which Jeanne would have to take into account if she wanted to add her efforts to the concert of the locally well-disposed, and at the same time safeguard the independence needed for the evangelical activities which she wished to pursue.

She arrived in Dinan on 4 August with Marie Jamet. For the time being, the town put one of the old bastions of the city-wall at her disposal, at the Porte de Brest. It was an unhealthy and inconvenient place, formerly used as a prison. Armed with permission from the authorities, they collected with success: a thousand francs in a few days.

Ever resourceful, Jeanne devised a new method to make collecting easier. She opened a subscription-book, in which

people put their names down to pay so much a month.
Thus, Mgr de Lesquen, formerly Bishop of Rennes, now
living in retirement in Dinan, undertook to subscribe ten
francs.

After the first three weeks, there were already six old
women; little by little the former prison filled up.

On 22 August, the poor refuge at Dinan was visited by
an English tourist, who was himself anxious to help the
aged. He later published an article describing his visit. He
wrote:

> To reach the floor where they were living, you had to negotiate
> an awkward spiral stair; the ceiling of the room was low, the
> walls were bare and rough, the windows narrow and grilled,
> so that you might have imagined you were in a cavern or a
> prison; but this dismal look was to some extent enlivened by
> the firelight and the happy appearance of the people inside . . .
>
> Jeanne received us kindly . . . She was simply but cleanly
> dressed in a black dress and white cap and kerchief; this is
> the dress adopted by the community. She looks about fifty
> years old, is of medium height with a sunburnt complexion,
> she looks worn out though her expression is serene and full of
> kindness; there is not the slightest trace of pretentiousness or
> conceit detectable in it . . .

A veritable interview then took place between the tourist—himself a person of standing, at the time busily preparing to found a hospice for the aged—and our Jeanne
Jugan. She gave straightforward answers to his questions.

> She never knew on any given day, she said, where the next
> day's provisions would come from, but she persevered, in the
> firm conviction that God would never abandon the poor, and
> acted according to this certain principle: that everything we
> do for them, we do for Our Lord Jesus Christ.
>
> I asked her how she could tell which were the ones truly
> deserving to be helped; she replied that she admitted those
> who applied to her and seemed to be the most destitute; that

she began with the aged and infirm as being those most in need; and that she used to make enquiries from their neighbours as to their character, means, &c.

Rather than leave those idle who could still set their hand to something useful, she made them unravel and card old bits of material, and then spin the wool thus recovered; by such means they are able to earn six *liards* a day . . . They also did other work as occasion would allow and received a third of the small return obtained.

Jeanne then described what she might expect from various tradespeople: foodstuffs still fit to eat but not so easy to sell.

I told her [the Englishman went on] that having covered France, she ought to come to England and teach us how to care for our own poor people. She replied that, with God's help, she would do so if invited.

There is something so calm, so holy about this woman that, seeing her, I felt as though I were in the presence of a higher being, and her words went so much to my heart that my eyes—I know not why—filled with tears.

That is Jeanne Jugan, the friend of the Brittany poor, and the sight of her alone would be enough to compensate for the horrors of a day and a night spent on the stormy sea.'

Like Monsieur Chevremont before him, our tourist and reporter had been struck by Jeanne's serenity.

And this is all the more remarkable since she was always active, always on the go, her brain just as alert as her limbs. At the time, she was looking for a house, for from the earliest days it was obvious that they could not go on living in that old tower. For twenty-four thousand francs, she bought a tumbledown former convent, from which the Capuchins had been expelled in 1791. It was, however, being occupied by a farmer and his lease still had another three years to run. Something else had to be found in the meantime; she rented a house in the Rue Saint-Marc.

These premises were unfurnished. To begin with, they slept on palliasses. Gifts arrived little by little. A doctor offered twelve wooden beds, a cow and some buckwheat. One day, a *good woman* was brought in; there were no more blankets available. One of the Sisters was just going to fetch her own to give her when a parcel arrived: it contained nine white blankets straight from the factory. When winter set in, a charitable person gave peat to fuel the stove. The different foundations helped one another: the Rennes community, which was better off, sent three dozen pairs of stockings for the *good women*.

They also had to share staff: two young Sisters came from Saint-Servan, and Virginie Trédaniel left Rennes to be appointed Superior of the community at Dinan.

Jeanne went on collecting. The memory was long preserved of her visit to the college 'Les Cordeliers' at Dinan where, as at Redon, she made a personal appeal to the senior pupils. They were also assured the *left-overs* from the hospital of the Brothers of St John of God, which housed 224 sick.

But as far as collecting was concerned, there was a new situation to be faced: the municipality wished to organise a Welfare Office and give it a regular income. For a time, Jeanne stopped collecting inside the town and hence was obliged to collect in the countryside or other districts. We know that during this period she went to beg alms from the spectators at the Cancale regatta (12 September 1846). Did she take the opportunity of visiting her old home? She also went to the steeplechases at Saint-Malo and the regatta at Saint-Suliac. She even considered going to England. And in any case certainly paid a visit to Jersey and spent about a fortnight collecting there. The poor had to live; nothing stopped her.

Then we see her leave Dinan for Rennes, where she was to spend a few weeks. She begged as she went, gathering up humble things: '*filasse*, ·wool, old stockings'. We find traces of her at Saint-Méen, Montauban, Montfort, Bédée.[1] She went back to Dinan towards the end of November and left almost immediately for Saint-Brieuc. The Mayor, to whom she first presented herself, thenceforth held the arm-chair in veneration, in which she had sat. On 10 January, readers of the *Publicateur des Côtes-du-Nord* were informed that

> Jeanne Jugan, the woman so devoted to the service of the unfortunate, who has worked miracles of charity and about whom the Breton press had so much to say last year, is now within our walls. She is making a collection for her work. Visiting charitable people, she merely says, 'I am *Jeanne Jugan*.' The name alone is enough to open all purses.

This collection brought in one thousand, five hundred francs. Was it at about this time that she visited the senior seminary at Saint-Brieuc? A pupil of the day, who later became a Jesuit, left a record of the visit. 'We heard her speak to us', he wrote, 'in tones of faith which pierced us to the quick.'

Her stay in Saint-Brieuc was also to be the occasion of a useful meeting; Monsieur du Clésieux, who had just opened a sort of orphanage for boys at Saint-Ilan (a work which was later taken over by the Congregation of the Holy Ghost Fathers), was in touch with Monsieur Dupont. Jeanne asked him to take on the handful of little boys still being looked after in the house at Saint-Servan and those whom she might gather up in the future, whether in the streets of Rennes or elsewhere. M. du Clésieux consented and wrote to tell M. Dupont, who in turn wrote to the Abbé Le Pailleur, 'Jeanne is very happy about this arrange-

---

[1] Reported by Sr Marie de la Conception (Eulalie Jamet) in a letter of 13 November 1846.

ment and, to the eye of faith, it is indeed something to rejoice over' (22 January).

Jeanne was happy about it because this agreement made it possible to put an end to a somewhat difficult situation which had lasted for five years: the presence of these little children at close quarters with the aged in the Saint-Servan house. She had taken them in because no suffering left her indifferent, and no doubt also because M. Le Pailleur was keen to widen the objectives of the work. But she knew, more and more clearly, that her particular mission was to house the aged poor.

SOURCES FOR CHAPTER 17

MANUSCRIPT SOURCES

Archives des Petites Sœurs des Pauvres. Letters and fragments of the first Little Sisters of the Poor : Marie Jamet, Eulalie Jamet, Virginie Trédaniel.

Testimony : Sœur Anne Auguste reported by Sœur Anne de la Nativité, Sœur Anne-Marie reported by the Abbé Leroy, Mrs Anderson reported by Sœur Agnès Onésime, Mlle Bétrel reported by Sœur Donatienne de Marie, Mme Gillet reported by Sœur Louise de l'Immaculée, Fr Lucas (Eudist) reported by Sœur Marguerite de la Visitation, Fr Monjarret, S. J. reported by Sœur Marie-Yvonne de Sainte Agnès and Sœur Aldegonde de la Providence.

Livre de fondation of the Dinan house. A. Leroy, *Détails complémentaires* . . . op. cit. Legal documents.

Bibliothèque municipale de Dinan. De L'Hommeau, *Histoire du vieux Dinan*, op. cit.

Archives de l'Oratoire de la Sainte-Face (Tours). Correspondence of M. Dupont.

PRINTED SOURCES CONTEMPORARY WITH JEANNE JUGAN

The translation of 'the English tourist's article' will be found in A.-L. Masson, *Les premières Petites Sœurs des Pauvres*, Lyon, Vitte, 1899, A. Leroy, *Histoire des Petites Sœurs des Pauvres*, op. cit. See Appendix I, *Printed Sources contemporary with Jeanne Jugan's life*, No. 1.

J. Lesage, *Mémoires. Coup d'œil rétrospectif sur la ville de Dinan depuis l'établissement de sa municipalité jusqu'à nos jours*, Dinan, Bazouge, 1871.

Newspaper articles: *Le Dinannais*, 16 August, 6 September, 1 November and 27 December 1846; 3 January 1847; *L'Impartial de Bretagne*, 11 September 1846; 15 January 1847; *Le Messager breton*, 25 June, 6 August, 3 September, 29 October, 17 and 31 December 1846; *Le Publicateur des Côtes-du-Nord*, 22 August, 5 and 12 September 1846; 9 January 1847. *Etrennes dinannaises*, first year (1848), Dinan, Huart.

LATER STUDIES

C. de La Corbinière, op. cit.
A. Leroy, op. cit.

18

ON THE ROADS

(1847–8)

For two years (1847–8), Jeanne went from town to town, incessantly collecting, at all times ready to answer appeals for help from her sisters. Totally available and disinterested.

She often travelled on foot, and the road was part of the background to her life, her thought, her prayer. And a place of testing, too, for the roads of France were not easy. This is how an economist described the better of these roads in 1830:

> Wide avenues, usually straight . . . cobbled or metalled (i.e. of stone chippings) down the middle but along so narrow a strip that two vehicles often barely have room to pass each other. This strip, although the best part of the road, is often neither solid nor flat; if metalled, it is full of pot-holes; if paved, it is hard and bumpy. It has the further defect of being too high in relation to the hard-shoulder, so that vehicles often have to take the greatest precautions in getting on and getting off it, or risk turning over. The hard-shoulders so-called are worse still: normally made of clay and washed over by the rainwater running off the middle part of the road into the ditches, they are no more, depending on the season, than a mass of dust or mud.

True, since the beginning of the reign of Louis-Philippe, many roads had been rebuilt, but the day of the tarmac surface had not yet dawned. And Jeanne often had to follow ways much muddier than these.

On them, she would meet other pedestrians, and they were not always very reassuring: tramps, beggars, soldiers, pedlars, not to mention brigands. No pavements in built-up areas or on bridges: accidents were common. You had to look out for yourself when a heavy *diligence* went by, or the big four-wheeler stage-coaches; or when the express mail-coach was overtaking the slower-moving local traffic. You also met many people travelling on horseback, and strings of pack-horses transporting goods from one place to another. After any journey on the roads, you invariably arrived covered in dust or caked in mud.

And that was how Jeanne went, 'her wallet slung across her shoulder and her basket over her arm', begging on behalf of the aged poor, or sometimes on her way to help one of the recently founded houses which was on the rocks.

For although the work was no longer hers, on several occasions she had to save it from disaster, since she was the one whom people were prepared to trust and since she was the one who could see what needed to be done. She would arrive, take the necessary decisions, obtain the funds that were lacking, encourage this person and that, then disappear; other people needed her. She had 'nowhere to rest her head'; she did not seem to belong to any particular local community. Nothing for herself, everything for the aged poor; with them she shared everything. For them to be housed, cared for, loved, she consented to be without hearth and home herself.

From Rennes, on 27 March 1847, Eulalie had written to her sister,

> People don't want to give to us any more; collecting brings in nothing. Since 1 January we have spent more than we have received . . . My good Mother, everyone is asking for Jeanne. I don't know whether they will give more readily, for people

have been upset by Monseigneur [a reference to Mgr Brossais Saint-Marc's severe attitude after the Abbé Le Pailleur's departure for Bougligny]. Françoise [Trévily] is in good health and is much liked in Rennes. Mother Virginie [Trédaniel, then Superior at Dinan] tells me that if Jeanne were to come to Rennes, she would ask for Françoise [to be sent to Dinan]. I do not think that this would be a good idea, but I am ready and willing to give her up if you wish.

We do not in fact know whether Jeanne went to Rennes or not; we lose track of her in 1847. But in the Saint-Servan *foundation-book*, we read: 'The collections were not bad. Sister Mary of the Cross divided her efforts according to the necessities of the various houses, going where the need for her presence was most felt.'

It was perhaps about now that she went to Vannes. There she paid a collecting visit to the de Chappotin family, where there were three little girls. Hélène, who was seven or eight, wanted to give her whole money-box. 'Five francs is enough,' said her mother. 'Which of you three is going to be a nun one day?' Jeanne asked. 'Not me,' said Hélène, 'I don't want to leave Mamma!' Jeanne then said, 'Those who say, *I should like to have a vocation* but will not give themselves, are not for God. But the one who says, *I don't want to*, is already stirred by grace.' It was prophetic: Hélène de Chappotin was to found the Congregation of the Franciscan Missionaries of Mary. On a number of occasions Jeanne similarly foretold lives to be consecrated to the Gospel. A little later, when she was covering the region of Chartres, she came to a family where the mother was anxious about her very difficult son: could he ever be a priest, as he said he wanted? 'Don't worry, Madame, your son will be a priest, though there will be many difficulties first.' He did, in fact, become one.

During one of her stays at Saint-Servan, Jeanne went to spend a day at the docks in the port of Saint-Malo. There

she met the Comte de Gouyon de Beaufort, in whose house
she had worked long before. He was a shipowner, his
vessels carrying the trade for a marine agency. He was a
very violent-tempered man, but Jeanne used to say that
during his fits of rage was when she got the most out of
him. She was in fact the only person to have any influence
over this fiery and explosive character. It happened, on the
day in question, that Monsieur de Gouyon was watching
the goods being off-loaded from one of his ships. Among
these were gold ingots done up in little bags, each containing the equivalent value of ten thousand francs. During the
unloading, one of the bags fell into the water. Furious anger
on the part of the shipowner—and just at this moment
Jeanne came along. Seeing him, she went up to him to find
out what had put him in a rage. She calmed him down by
promising to pray for the lost money to be recovered, and
went on her way. They managed to fish the bag out of the
water, and Jeanne came by again soon afterwards; her
former employer was in fact holding the dripping bag in
his hands. 'I told you, dear Monsieur de Gouyon, that God
would make you recover your money!' Prompted now by
his natural kindness, the shipowner threw the bag of gold
into Jeanne's arms, saying, 'Here, take the bag; this is for
your little old folk!'

Monsieur de Gouyon was a loyal friend to the Saint-
Servan house. He often used to send offerings for the aged.
For instance, some deliveries of salt bacon which were to
have been taken aboard his ships, were not up to standard;
he refused to accept them and sent the home 1220 pounds
of bacon. This unexpected stock came like a fortune and
the Sisters knew exactly what to do with it.

At the end of 1847, the Sisters of the Poor held their first
'chapter'; it consisted of the Superiors of the four houses:
Saint-Servan, Rennes, Dinan and Tours. Jeanne was not
invited to it. The meeting was probably presided over by

the Abbé Le Pailleur, for it was at about this time that he came back from Bougligny to give retreats: not having received his permits from Mgr Brossais Saint-Marc, who was still angry with him, he gave his retreats in Dinan.

At this time, the *little work*, as it was called, consisted of nine Sisters of the Poor, nine novices and a few postulants. New recruits received a summary training; it took place almost entirely 'on the shop-floor' under the charge of Marie Jamet and the very young Sister Pauline (Joséphine Denieul, born in 1830); the parish clergy helped with it a little. The young candidates were given a few months' grounding in prayer, the rule and the common life, and were then sent to the houses. From time to time, one of the three Bougligny priests would come and give a retreat, or preside over ceremonies of clothing or profession.

In February 1848 when the revolution occurred which gave birth to the Second Republic, Jeanne was in Rennes. Brittany remained calm. The change of government came as a complete surprise there. Jeanne did not interrupt her collecting; pictures have come to light which she gave her benefactors exactly at that time, and which bear her name and the date.

In April, she was urgently recalled to Dinan. We learn this from the following letter addressed from Saint-Servan by Virginie Trédaniel to Marie in faraway Tours:

> I have received a letter from Dinan: the Sisters are well but the collections are a failure, not bringing in a penny. And Claire [who was in charge there, aged 22 and only admitted a few months previously!] tells me that she has no money left in the house; she asks for Sister Jeanne. She tells me that the principal benefactors have lost confidence; they think the house will collapse if Jeanne does not go there . . . I am writing to Rennes today to ask for Jeanne to go and do a round in Dinan.

Always available, Jeanne answered the summons, without difficulty regaining the confidence of the friends of the poor; the result of her collecting made it possible for the debts to be paid off and a few provisions to be laid in. More important: she was able to restore and tighten the bonds of friendship without which the house could not survive. For a long while afterwards, the people of Dinan felt a need to remind themselves that Jeanne was still the real guarantor of the work; until 1855, they continued knowing her as the *Lady Principal of the Home for the Aged*. It was the same in the diocese of Saint-Brieuc: here the parish priest of Dinan applied for permission to celebrate Mass in the home at the end of 1849 'on behalf of the Lady Superior of the Religious of Jeanne Jugan'; the authorisation was entered under the heading, *Oratory of the Jeanne Jugan Ladies at Dinan*.

At the end of June 1848, Paris had known days of bloodshed. The city was divided, the working-class quarters in the east against the middle-class areas in the west: scenes of civil war. Taking fright, the National Assembly enacted laws shackling the popular Press and freedom of association. In an article commenting on these actions, Lamennais exclaimed with doleful irony, 'Let the poor shut up!' In this same period, Jeanne, never weakening, lent them her voice too: a tireless collector, at once discreet and bold, never ceasing to probe the consciences of her fellow-citizens on their behalf.

On 3 February 1849 she was back collecting in Saint-Brieuc with the warm encouragement of the Bishop. But she only stayed there for a few days; in difficulties, the house at Tours was urgently calling for her help.

SOURCES FOR CHAPTER 18

MANUSCRIPT SOURCES

Archives des Petites Sœurs des Pauvres. Letters and fragments of the first Little Sisters of the Poor : Marie Jamet, Eulalie Jamet, Virginie Trédaniel.

Testimony : Abbé J.-B. Briand, Comtesse de la Haye Saint-Hilaire, Abbé J. Genty reported by Sœur Antoinette de Saint Berchmans, Sœur Noël de Saint Alfred and Sœur Françoise de l'Annonciation.

Livres de fondation of the Dinan, Rennes and Saint-Servan houses. Holy pictures signed by Jeanne Jugan. A. Leroy, *Détails complémentaires* . . . op. cit.

Archives de l'évêché de Saint-Brieuc. Administrative records.

PRINTED SOURCES CONTEMPORARY WITH JEANNE JUGAN

Newspaper, *Le peuple constituant,* 11 July 1848.

Etrennes dinannaises, consacrées aux intérêts administratifs, industriels et historiques de l'arrondissement de Dinan, for the year 1849 (p. 77); 1852 (p. 11); 1853, 1854, 1855.

LATER STUDIES

M. Agulhon, *1848, ou l'apprentissage de la République,* Paris, Seuil, 1973.

J. Delumeau, op. cit.

G. Goyau, *Une fondatrice missionnaire, Mère Marie de la Passion, et les Franciscaines missionnaires de Marie,* Paris, Spes, 1935.

R. Héron de Villefosse, *Histoire des grandes routes de France,* Paris, Librairie académique Perrin, 1975.

A. Leroy, op. cit.

J. Vidalenc, op. cit.

19

TOURS

(1849)

The foundation at Tours had been made without Jeanne Jugan, two years earlier. In brief, this is how.

A long while before, Monsieur Dupont had expressed a desire to see the Little Sisters come to Tours, and his invitations became more and more pressing. A lady in Tours, Mademoiselle Chicoisneau de La Valette, who was related to people in Saint-Servan, was all ready to help the Sisters.

Eventually, in January 1847, Monsieur Dupont wrote, 'The Little Sisters of the Poor, those noble emulators of Jeanne Jugan, have arrived . . . The work of these excellent women is destined to spread everywhere.' In a word, Marie Jamet, one novice and one postulant had taken up quarters under his roof.

They then rented a house in the parish of La Riche. M. Dupont presented three beds: one in his own name, one in his mother's and one in his daughter's. For the first few days the house stood empty. On the evening of the feast of the Epiphany, the three Sisters were having supper with M. Dupont; they were sad at not having any old people. As they were beginning their meal, the doorbell rang: an old woman was waiting for them at the La Riche house. They rushed there and gave her a warm welcome. (Apparently the dinner had followed them there.) By the end of the month there were fifteen old women there.

On 9 January 1847, they began collecting. A Sister, accompanied by Mlle de La Valette, went begging for the poor. On 10 January, the *Journal d'Indre-et-Loire* announced this on its front page. It introduced the Sisters who, it said, 'belong to an association known as the Jeanne Jugan Association'; it also printed Dupin's discourse to the Academy. Dupin was still opening doors more than a year after the event!

Mgr Morlot, the Archbishop, had shown some initial reserve, but began to take an interest in the Sisters' work and even pushed them, a little later, into acquiring an enormous house which happened to be empty: the former mother-house of the Sisters of the Presentation. And he let it be known that *it would not displease him to see* the mother-house and novitiate installed in it. (He had perhaps got wind of the troubles which had arisen at Rennes after the Abbé Le Pailleur's departure for Bougligny.)

And so it came about that, thanks to a sum of twenty thousand francs given by M. Dupont from the dowry of his beloved daughter who had just died, they bought this house and moved into it in February 1848.

At the end of the same year, the mother-house and novitiate were moved there. The house at Saint-Servan had become much too small to accommodate the fifteen or so postulants and novices who were now preparing to become Little Sisters. The Congregation's growth had begun; it was to expand very rapidly. A year later (August 1849), there were to be forty novices and postulants at Tours.[1]

A few weeks before the novices arrived, the house at Tours was visited by a man whose voice was to make Jeanne Jugan's name famous: Louis Veuillot.

Veuillot, editor-in-chief of *L'Univers* since 1843, had been converted to the Christian faith ten years before and

---

[1] The novitiate, numbering fourteen or fifteen at the beginning of 1849, was more than double the size by the end of the summer.

pledged his great talents to the fiery and intransigent service of the Gospel. In Tours lived one of the editors of
L'Univers, Léon Aubineau. As president of the local branch
of the Society of St Vincent de Paul, he knew the Sisters
well, and it was almost certainly he who took Veuillot to
visit them. Veuillot interviewed the Superior, Marie Jamet,
and what he later published in *L'Univers* was a direct echo
of what Marie Jamet herself had told him. (We shall see
how, much later, the Abbé Le Pailleur was to give him a
very different version of the facts.)

On his return to Paris, early in September 1848, Veuillot
attended a debate in the National Assembly on *the right to
assistance* written into the preamble to the new Constitution:
'The Republic ought . . . by brotherly assistance to safeguard the lives of needy citizens, be it by providing them
with work according to the measure of its resources, or by
coming to the help of those who are unfit to work and have
no family to support them.' On leaving the chamber, Veuillot, who had little faith in the progress of human society
and little sympathy with republican or socialist ideas, wrote
a resounding article about Jeanne Jugan and her work. In
it, he explained to the deputies that he was going to tell
them about 'someone more versed in socialism than the lot
of you'. (This polemical approach was not, we may think,
notably faithful either to Jeanne Jugan's spirit or
intentions.)

Here are a few of his remarks,

> She loved the poor because she loved God. One day she
> begged her confessor to teach her how to love God even more.
> 'Jeanne,' he said, 'up to now you have been giving to the poor;
> from now on, you must share with them.' . . . That same
> evening, Jeanne had a companion, or rather a mistress.
>
> I saw clean clothes, happy faces, and even radiant health.
> Between the youthful Sisters and these old people reigns a
> mutual affection and respect to gladden the heart . . .

The nuns conform in every respect to the regime of their poor people, and there is no difference whatever, except that the Sisters serve and the poor are served. . . . Everything happens pat for the needs of the moment. At supper, nothing is left over; at dinner, nothing is lacking. Charity provided the house. When a new inmate turns up, charity provides a bed and clothes.

At the beginning of his article, Veuillot noted, 'I have had the privilege of seeing the Reverend Mother-General; this is not Jeanne Jugan. That illustrious woman stays at their house at Saint-Servan and is only second in the family which she has brought into existence.'

In fact, as we have seen, she was not often at Saint-Servan. In 1846 she was in Rennes, then in Dinan. In 1847 and 1848 she was going from town to town. Then in February 1849, summoned by her sisters, she went to Tours. The principal matter in hand was to obtain official authorisations, which had not been given.

M. Dupont was carried away with excitement.

For the last two days we have been honoured to have with us Jeanne Jugan, the mother of all the Little Sisters . . . What admirable trust in God! What love for his Holy Name! She will do much good for us at Tours. Benighted worldlings suppose that this *poor beggar-maid*, as she calls herself, will ask them for alms; but if their eyes were opened, they too would understand that they receive a greater alms from her by hearing her speak so lovingly and simply about God's Providence.

This letter is not merely enthusiastic; with profound and accurate insight, it presents one of the major axes of Jeanne Jugan's life, highlighting its apostolic scope. Jeanne can talk 'so lovingly and simply about God's Providence' because she lives by it, she has thrown in her lot with Him who wished the Glad Tidings to be preached to the poor. She makes no conscious attempt 'to convert people'; she

bears witness, with no ulterior motive, because God's charity dwells in her and she puts it into action. Her witness
was amplified by the voices of others, by Veuillot for
instance, or even by Dupin senior, and then, as we shall
see, by Charles Dickens, who between them gave her a
vast audience.

On reaching Tours, Jeanne there met a young man
called Hector d'Outremont, a very active member of the
local branch of the Society of St Vincent de Paul. She told
him about the early years of her work, and M. d'Outremont
wrote all this down. His account later passed into the
possession of the Little Sisters of the Poor, where unfortunately it was destroyed. The authoress of its destruction
afterwards made known her regret. M. d'Outremont later
became a priest and Bishop of Le Mans, and was to be an
efficacious friend to the Little Sisters.

The youthful Sister Pauline wrote from Tours to the
Abbé Le Pailleur on 19 February 1849, telling him about
the visits she had paid to their benefactors and to the
Bishop, accompanied by *Sister Jeanne*. (From which it is
clear that at this point the name Sister Mary of the Cross
had not yet become current, even inside the Congregation,
or even with young Sisters who had entered it long after it
had started.) Then they had been to see the parish priest,
who had advised them to go back and see the Bishop again
and ask him for a letter of recommendation to the clergy.
They had gone to him.

> Monseigneur told her that he did not dare to move too fast.
> She went down on her knees, she left him entirely free to
> decide as his great charity might dictate. He was touched by
> this and told her to wait a few days and he would do it . . .
> We only wish that M. d'Outremont were in Tours, to get him
> to put a word or two in the paper about Sister Jeanne. She
> tells me that this would be very useful, and that she has been

into several shops and found people as hard-hearted as brooms . . .

We have been to see the Prefect's lady, who received us kindly and the same evening sent us a permit for the whole Department from her husband, whom we had not been able to see . . .

I am very happy to have Sister Jeanne, she is very kind, she likes it here at Tours but is a little upset at the thought of still not being able to go collecting . . .

I think Sister Catherine will be suitable to go collecting. Sister Jeanne likes her very much.

This letter allows us a vivid glimpse of how Jeanne was behaving in her Congregation ten years after its inception, and how a young Sister might see her. In point of fact, Jeanne was to leave the house at Tours on a solid footing, well rooted in the hearts of the people there.

But already the joyful news generated by this evangelical dynamism was spreading further afield. M. d'Outremont told his fellow-members of the Society of St Vincent de Paul in Paris about what was going on in Tours. And these then asked for a house to be founded in Paris. Marie Jamet went to Saint-Servan to make preparations for it at the beginning of 1849. She came back to Tours on 9 March with Sister Marie-Louise, and the two of them set off for Paris on 28 March. The first house in Paris was founded on 1 August.

A letter arrived, too, from Besançon: a certain Mademoiselle Junot had seen about *Jeanne Jugan's work* in Veuillot's article and asked for a house to be set up there. In November, Sister Pauline left Tours for Besançon and had Jeanne's Montyon Award publicised there. In Tours, she had gained her experience with Jeanne present; now she was to organise the foundation at Besançon. The same year, a house was opened in Nantes at the request of the members of the Society of St Vincent de Paul. It was at

Nantes that the name *Little Sisters of the Poor* became current;[2] folk-wisdom had hit on the epithet most aptly expressing Jeanne Jugan's intention: excluding all domination, to become little so as to love more.

SOURCES FOR CHAPTER 19

MANUSCRIPT SOURCES

Archives des Petites Sœurs des Pauvres. Letters and fragments of the first Little Sisters of the Poor : Marie Jamet, Sœur Pauline. Note of Sœur Alexis de Sainte-Thérèse. Testimony of Sœur Apollinaire du Saint-Sacrement. A. Helleu, *Note et observations . . .* op. cit.

A. Leroy, *Détails complémentaires . . . Livre de fondation* of the Tours house.

Archives de l'Oratoire de la Sainte-Face (Tours). Correspondence of M. Dupont.

PRINTED SOURCES CONTEMPORARY WITH JEANNE JUGAN

Constitution de la République française, 1848. *Journal d'Indre-et-Loire,* 10 January 1847; 27 September 1848. *L'Univers,* 13 September 1848.

LATER STUDIES

P. D. Janvier, *Vie de M. Dupont . . .* op. cit.
A. Leroy, op. cit.

---

[2] Actually the expression *Little Sisters of the Poor* appears in one of the Abbé Le Pailleur's letters as early as 10 September 1847, 'A number of young women of social standing are enduring persecution from their families . . . This is because they want to become Little Sisters of the Poor.' But it was only in 1849 that the name became, first popular, then official.

20

AT ANGERS

(1849–51)

Jeanne was collecting: this is our constant refrain.

In 1849 she trekked through Touraine, Beauce and Anjou. Léon Aubineau says of her at about this time, 'She goes everywhere. Perhaps you will see her coming through your door, to explain the reason for her visit with dignified simplicity—the needs of her poor—and to speak of the Lord's mercies to them.'

She collected in thanksgiving, her heart overflowing with the misery of the poor, yet marvelling at such love lavished by God.

No period of her active life was more joyous, more lyrical, than those weeks of her collecting in Anjou and of the subsequent foundation.

She arrived at the beginning of December 1849; a number of families more or less connected with the Society of St Vincent de Paul were eagerly awaiting her. In particular, she was to be adopted by Monsieur and Madame de Quatrebarbes and by Mademoiselle Zénobie de Caqueray.

Entirely devoted to serving God and the poor, the latter introduced her to members of the clergy. In exchange, she asked her for one present: her collecting basket. (Was it still the one which Brother Claude-Marie Gandet had given her in 1841? Surely she must have worn out several since!) Mlle de Caqueray gave her a new one. And herself left a description of this venerable object, now unfortunately lost, 'of medium size, closed with a lid fastened near the handle and opening in a semi-circle when raised at either end. Originally the wicker of which it was made must have been white, but when I knew it the effects of time had turned it to the colour of ripe wheat.'

The Quatrebarbes, too, were valued friends. A humble man, the Count was absolutely devoted to the poor. His wife is related to have laughingly said to him one day, 'My dear, if it wasn't for me, you would end up with no other home but the hospice!' 'That would suit me fine,' he replied, 'for there I should have my best friends for company, I mean the Sisters and the poor. Besides,' he added with his reputedly irresistible smile, 'besides, you would come and see me from time to time, I hope!' He was created to get on well with Jeanne. So he took her with him in his carriage or his brougham, and made her do a tour of the great houses of Anjou, so that she would be known in them and might call again on her own. She was as much at ease in these, as much her simple self, as among her poor or in government offices.

Thus it was that she visited the Château du Bourg-d'Iré, the home of old Madame de Falloux whose son had been appointed Minister of Education the previous year; he was to be a loyal friend to Jeanne. Twenty-five years later, in 1874, he was to remind her, when she was very old herself, of this first visit in Anjou—followed soon after by his mother's death.[1]

In Angers, Jeanne was collecting for foundations already made. But from the outset she had in mind (as in Rennes) to open a house in Angers, where she had been given so warm a welcome. In its streets she met beggars, of whom there had been so many since the beginning of the century.

[1] Mme de Falloux died on 6 December 1850. Fr Lelièvre, describing M. de Falloux's visit to La Tour in 1874, notes that he saw Jeanne, 'admired her eighty-two years, her fine bearing, her white stick.' But we anticipate.

She knew that the Welfare Office could never cope with all that needed to be done. Indeed, industrialisation, which accentuated the poverty in Angers, was to develop even faster in the next few years—fifteen years later, eight thousand out of some fifty thousand inhabitants were to have their names on the Welfare Office books; but already there was plenty of hardship to relieve, particularly that endured by the aged poor. There was indeed, as in Rennes, a civil hospice for the bedridden aged, and the Sisters of Sainte-Marie d'Angers did what they could there to mitigate the misery characterising the hospitals of the period; there was also a poor-house founded in 1831 by the combined efforts of charitable individuals and later taken over by the municipality, which accommodated about a hundred more or less delinquent beggars of all ages and humanely did its best to rehabilitate them.

Other old people—only to mention these—could count on limited assistance from a number of organisations to which charitable resourcefulness had given rise: some ladies had formed a group called the 'Guild of the Nativity', to visit the poor; others had formed an 'Association of Ladies of Providence', for any kind of charitable work; the local branch of the Society of St Vincent de Paul, founded in 1838, had a young and active membership and had opened a clothing-centre. All this was already in existence and working well, and it may be that at Angers charity seemed less ineffectual against poverty than elsewhere. Even so, Jeanne was very much aware that many of the aged poor needed to be admitted to, and loved in, a house meant especially for them.

She talked about this to friends of hers in Angers and found them very ready to co-operate. On 11 December, Monsieur Maupoint, a Vicar-General of Rennes, paid a visit to the Little Sisters of that city; although he had not made their acquaintance before, he had received a request from Angers: would he agree to give a house and chapel which he owned there, to the aged poor? It seems he was pleased with his visit to the Sisters in Rennes, for this was the start of a long friendship, while his chapel and house in Angers were in fact to become the first home for the Sisters and their old folk in that city.

The foundation was made in April 1850. During the previous winter months, Jeanne had presumably gone back to Tours with the proceeds of her collecting; she then had to go begging in other regions.

So on Wednesday 3 April, Marie Jamet, Sister Pauline and Sister Félicité de Sainte Marie left Tours, accompanied by Jeanne, to open the home in Angers. Mgr Angebault, the Bishop, received them with open arms and handed them the keys of Monsieur Maupoint's chapel. He said to Marie, 'Now, my daughter, open your doors to all the poor people who are asking for you, and do good.' As elsewhere, they arrived empty handed: the four of them had only six francs between them to open the establishment.

Jeanne applied for the permits to go collecting, and these were drawn up in her name. Hers were the activities reported in the newspapers. In Angers, as at Saint-Servan, the Sisters were often to be called *the Jeanne Jugans*. The *Journal de Maine-et-Loire* of 12 April reported as follows,

> Three months ago, Jeanne Jugan was collecting from us . . . The good reception which she had here touched her heart. 'I am now in debt to the people of Angers,' she said when she left. 'I shall soon come and pay it back.'
>
> As good as her word, the kind-hearted Breton is now within our walls. . . . This is the letter of introduction which she presented to our municipality:[2]
>
> *Our origin is explained in Monsieur Dupin's discourse concerning the Montyon Award; since this piece of encouragement, God has blessed*

---

[2] Style and errors of chronology in the list of foundations alike suggest that this collective letter had certainly not been drawn up by the Little Sisters of the Poor.

us. We are eighty Sisters; we house, feed and nurse from five to six hundred infirm old people in seven houses, successively established at Saint-Servan, Dinan, Rennes, Nantes, Tours, Paris and Besançon. In all these places, the support of the Bishops, the protection of the municipalities and the charity of the public have been all we needed. Our statutes are the fruit of experience, being inspired by the needs of the poor. A very simple rule, which consists in co-ordinating our various exercises, is our means of unity and activity.

Two days later, Marie left again for Tours, 'already consoled'. She took two postulants from Angers with her, and these no doubt had been making up their minds since Jeanne's first collecting round in December.

The Sisters, then, moved into the former chapel and set to work adapting it to their purpose. On 29 April, the first old people were admitted. Collecting yielded excellent results, especially in kind.

All the same, they were short of butter and Jeanne saw the old people eating dry bread. 'But this is the land of butter!' she exclaimed. 'Why on earth don't you ask St Joseph for some?' She lit a night-light in front of St Joseph's statue, had all the empty butter-dishes fetched and propped up a card: 'Good St Joseph, send us butter for our old folk!' Visitors were amazed or amused at such simplicity of heart; one of them expressed misgivings at the sight of the empty butter-dishes! But a few days later, an anonymous donor sent a very large amount of butter, and all the dishes were filled.

Jeanne wanted the atmosphere to be cheerful. On the strength of her friendly contacts in Anjou, she went somewhat timidly one day to see the colonel commanding one of the units of the Angers garrison and asked him to send some of the regimental bandsmen to make her old folk happy, one feast-day afternoon. 'Sister, to please you and make your beloved old folk happy, I'll send you the whole band.' The Angers brass-band provides a merry accompaniment to that self-giving love arousing love in others.

A Doctor Renier offered to treat the old people free. He belonged to the Society of St Vincent de Paul, as did a number of the most steadfast benefactors.

One of the members of this chain of mutual aid did more than give of his possessions: he offered himself. This was a young priest, Paul Gontard. Originally a lawyer, he had become more concerned with serving the Gospel and had been ordained in 1848. He presented a bed for the old people. Coming to the house in that part of the city called La Doutre, he was struck by the poverty of the Sisters and their joyful humility. And during that luminous summer of 1850, one fine day, he packed his bag, set off for Paris and went to the house in the Rue Saint-Jacques, where the Mother Superior-General then was; and pledged himself with all he had to the service of the Congregation, remaining there until his death in 1873. Other priests, as we shall see, were later to follow his example.[3]

About now, Jeanne left Angers to go begging through the other towns in the Department. She was provided with a permit from the Prefect, guaranteeing *the Lady Jeanne Jugan* the protection of the civil and military authorities throughout the Department. In Angers itself, collecting was to be taken over by a novice whom Jeanne had trained.

In Angers, Jeanne left a lasting memory behind her. One day, nearly thirty years later, Léon Cosnier, one of the people who had received her there, was passing a disorderly group of youngsters who were bawling bawdy songs. Suddenly, the Angelus rang out. One of the girls said to the others, 'That's Jeanne Jugan's little bell. She's listening to us.' Calm returned and the group dispersed.

In November 1850, the home sustained a severe shock.

[3] Fr Ernest Lelièvre, of whom we shall treat later, was one of these auxiliaries, clerical and lay. Their association never made much headway and was dissolved in 1896, the developing Congregation no longer needing their collaboration.

The very young Superior, Sister Félicité de Sainte-Marie, aged 23, died of typhoid fever; this was the first bereavement to occur in the family of the Little Sisters of the Poor. Sister Félicité was replaced by the novice who had been doing the collecting.

Keeping house in the Abbé Maupoint's chapel could not last; at best it was only a provisional solution. The place was badly ventilated. The Sisters' quarters were divided from the old people's ward by a paper partition. When an inmate had died, the body was moved into the Sisters' part where they kept vigil beside it during the night. On 24 December 1850, the community acquired a property called La Mélinais, on high ground just outside the city, and moved in shortly afterwards.

But Jeanne had already left Anjou. She was collecting.

About this time—the winter of 1850-1—a letter from Marie Jamet to the Superior at Dinan gives these clues to Jeanne's whereabouts, 'Tell Sister Mary of the Cross not to go collecting round Le Mans or in the Department of Mayenne, since we are about to start a foundation at Laval.' And a little later, 'She can go to Brest. We are pleased with the three girls whom she saw at Lorient.' Dinan, Lorient, Brest: a few milestones on Jeanne's travels. And wherever she went, she called others: a fair proportion of the first Little Sisters came forward to follow the same path as Jeanne, the path of poverty shared. In this way, too, she was *the mother of all the Little Sisters of the Poor*.

She stopped for a while in Dinan. A glimpse of her, evidently dating from this stay, has been preserved. In March 1851, a Monsieur Germainville came from Paris to found a branch of the Society of St Vincent de Paul in Dinan. He went to see the Little Sisters. Twelve years later, asking for Jeanne Jugan to make a new foundation in Paris for old soldiers, he was to recall the memory of his meeting with 'the Great Jugan ... I can still see her with your other Sisters, sitting back on their heels, singing hymns.'

But let us follow her to Brest. She rightly thought that in this town there were many poor forsaken old people. She began by seeking out a very active lady, the widow of a naval officer, Madame Thirat de Chailly, who had organised there a women's branch of the Society of St Vincent de Paul.

Their meeting was not encouraging. In the prevailing conditions, everything seemed weighted against such a plan, and the difficulties were insurmountable. Jeanne listened, understood. She thought for a while, then decided, 'Very well, dear lady, we'll try!'

She set about collecting. A friend went with her, Mademoiselle Chouteau. They came to a house where the latter expected to get a cold welcome; it would be wiser to leave it out. But Jeanne, grabbing the bell-rope, replied, 'We'll ring in God's name and God will bless us.' The donation was generous.

We'll ring in God's name. The formula perfectly expresses Jeanne's secret. Her work was not her own; it was God's. Her courage was not her own; it was Christ's strength. Boldness and freedom, trust and thanksgiving were the climate of her existence. And the secret of her happiness.

SOURCES FOR CHAPTER 20

MANUSCRIPT SOURCES

Archives des Petites Sœurs des Pauvres. Letters and fragments of the first Little Sisters of the Poor : Marie Jamet, Eulalie Jamet.

Testimony of Little Sisters of the Poor : Sœur Jeanne de l'Immaculée, Sœur Marie-Thérèse de Saint Pierre, Sœur Marie de Saint Laurent, Sœur Saint Albert, Sœur Maria de Sainte Luce.

Other testimony : Abbé Chauvin, Mlle Gicquel des Touches. Letter of M. Germainville. Permit of the Prefect of Maine-et-Loire. Legal documents. Holy pictures (Fourmy, Quatrebarbes, Ursulines de Jésus de Bellefontaine). Letters of Fr Lelièvre (8 August 1873, 1874).

Livre de fondation of the Angers house. A. Leroy, *Détails complémentaires . . .* op. cit.

PRINTED SOURCES CONTEMPORARY WITH JEANNE JUGAN

L. Aubineau, op. cit.

L. Cosnier, *Le dépôt de mendicité d'Angers. A MM. les conseillers généraux de Maine-et-Loire,* Angers, Imprimerie P. Lachèse, Belleuvre et Dolbeau, 1867.

Journal de Maine-et-Loire, 12 April and 18 December 1850.

LATER STUDIES

L. Cosnier, *La charité à Angers,* 2 vol., Angers, Lachèse, 1889–90.

A. Leroy, op. cit.

21

GROWTH

(1850–2)

During the summer of 1851, two retreats were held in Rennes at the Maison de la Madeleine. It seems likely that Jeanne took part in one of these gatherings. The Sisters of Angers preserved a record of them,

Having been summoned to Rennes, half of us went there for the first retreat, and the other half for the second one. There we found ourselves with our Little Sisters of the Brittany houses; eight days were spent in silence and recollection, entirely taken up with reviewing our obligations before God and with re-assuming with renewed resolve those sacrifices demanded by the hospitaller life. But the house in Rennes had so little room in it that we had to sleep in a loft which a lady living nearby allowed us to use. There we had the opportunity of practising poverty as the Divine Saviour practised it, and this gave us great joy. It was in July. There were thirty of us in this loft, on a scattering of straw, with a blanket or our clothes to cover us. Every now and then, we felt the rats scuttling over us, while the horses pawed in their stable down below. As regards food, the Superior of Rennes did everything she possibly could for no one to go short, but she had a hundred poor people to feed and her purse was never well lined.

This account gives us a picture of conditions obtaining in the *little family* at the time. No longer *the little work* of early days, there were now about ten houses. Soon there were to be more than a hundred Sisters, nearly all of them very young. They were still very poor, very dependent on the daily collection. Even so, the time had now come to get organised, to acquire an official existence in the Church, to become a proper *congregation*.

At Rennes, in the course of the difficulties of the previous years, Mgr Brossais Saint-Marc had made it very clear to the Sisters that they were not religious in the proper sense of the word; he had instructed the diocesan clergy to regard them as *good women*, not as *religious*. Nonetheless, they had their four vows . . . In their dilemma, they consulted the Bougligny priests, who replied that, for want of official approbation, these *vows* were only *private* and not *religious* ones.

Meanwhile a more uniform dress had been adopted, the cloak worn out of doors being part of it. To begin with, at Rennes, the hood was worn back on the shoulders; at Tours, it was habitually worn over the head, 'as the local women wear it; this usage was adopted in the little family.'

In February 1850, Eulalie wrote from Rennes, 'Monsieur Maupoint [Vicar-General of the Diocese] has just gone out of the house . . . He is more angry than I can describe at the novitiate's being at Tours. He said that Rennes was where it ought to be, "If I had been in the diocese sooner, I should never have allowed it to leave!" ' He and other priests had a word with the Bishop, and the latter gradually began to take a more favourable attitude.

Meanwhile, in the course of 1850, the Congregation continued to expand. After Angers, there were foundations at Bordeaux, Rouen and Nancy. In 1851, the novitiate was transferred from Tours to Paris.

That year also saw the first foundation made in England, in the suburbs of London. This foundation was much assisted by an article by Charles Dickens in his weekly *Household Words* (14 February 1852). In it he described a

visit to the home in Paris, which had made a deep impression on him. Beginning with a brief and very accurate
account of how the work began, he went on to describe the
house in the rue St Jacques, 'One old fellow has his feet
upon a little foot-warmer, and thinly pipes out that he is
very comfortable now, for he is always warm. The chills of
age and the chills of the cold pavement remain together in
his memory—but he is very comfortable now, very
comfortable.'

Growth went on at a great rate. In December 1851, there
were three hundred Sisters and fifteen houses harbouring
one thousand, five hundred old people. Eighteen months
later, there were five hundred Sisters. At her prayers,
Jeanne Jugan must have been dazzled by this fertility, by
such generosity on God's part.

It was now a matter of urgency to prepare draft constitutions, so that the association could obtain official approbation. Father Massot, who was implored to do this, set to
work. In April 1851, he invited the Abbé Le Pailleur to
stay with the Brothers of St John of God at Lille and there,
in isolation, they worked for three weeks.

Their draft was based on the text of 1846, while making
it less severe and prefacing it with a number of chapters
on training, practice of vows and structure of government.
The style got rid of the somewhat archaic phraseology of
the constitutions of the Hospitaller Order, but the latter
once and for all imbued the Little Sisters' future constitutions with its own far-ranging charity—for the Little Sisters' constitutions—like those of their model—adopted the
vow of hospitality.[1]

Such was the Rule of 1852. Once again, Father Félix
Massot, wise to the way Jeanne and her sisters had been
living, intervened decisively with his help. We can be sure

[1] See parallel texts of the two Rules at the end of this chapter.

that this help and the very imitation of the Brothers' constitutions reflected Jeanne's own deepest wish, as she had reposed such trust from the outset in Father Gandet and, later, in Father Massot himself.

With the Sisters' agreement, the draft was submitted to the Bishop of Rennes. The latter had it studied, so they say, by Monsieur Maupoint, his Vicar-General.

In the meantime, they were looking about for somewhere to fix the mother-house and novitiate. There was a property for sale on the outskirts of Rennes, called La Piletière; it was a spinning-mill on the verge of falling down. They bought it. Now it turned out that one of the joint-owners was Mgr Brossais Saint-Marc's mother. The Bishop, as Father Le Pailleur had anticipated, was very pleased with the transaction. The effects of this were that, not only did the Sisters get more spacious accommodation, but a reconciliation between the Abbé Le Pailleur, now permanently back from Bougligny, and his Bishop was brought nearer.

La Piletière had plenty of room in it; it was thought that it could shelter more people than the home at Rennes even when enlarged. And we learn from one of Marie Jamet's letters, 'Monsieur Maupoint has spoken to the Bishop about the novitiate and told him that Rennes had it filched away but that it would have to be given back; and that La Piletière would be very suitable for them . . . The Bishop kept saying, "Good, very good." ' The same day, Mgr Brossais Saint-Marc wrote a letter to Cardinal Fornari in Rome as the first step to procuring future approbation from the Pope. On 25 February 1852, Marie was announcing, 'Monseigneur would gladly have the novitiate, wanted no more than episcopal rights, agreed to the Rule and a Father Superior-General.' And forthwith, novices and postulants began to gather at La Piletière. The Mother Superior-General was also to take up residence there.

Eventually, on 29 May, Mgr Brossais Saint-Marc signed the decree approving the statutes. From then on, the family of the Little Sisters of the Poor was a proper religious congregation within the Church. And to emphasise his approval, the Bishop visited La Piletière two days later; there he presided over the clothing of twenty-four postulants and the profession of seventeen novices. In his sermon, he recalled God's providential acts in the history of the Little Sisters of the Poor from the day when he first paid them a visit 'in a little cellar' at Saint-Servan.

Thenceforth installed in the mother-house, the Abbé Le Pailleur had every reason to be satisfied: episcopal approval now made him officially the Father Superior-General of the Little Sisters of the Poor.

So, without further delay, he took a decision: he summoned the humble and indefatigable Jeanne Jugan to the mother-house. She was no longer to go collecting; she would no longer sustain her contacts with benefactors; she was to live out her life hidden behind the walls of La Piletière.

Jeanne obeyed. She came to live at the mother-house. She was never again to leave it, but remain in it until she died, twenty-seven years later.

Her visible task was done.

Here are the parallel texts of the two Rules:

CONSTITUTIONS OF THE BROTHERS OF SAINT JOHN OF GOD (1717)	RULE OF THE LITTLE SISTERS OF THE POOR (1852)
Our fourth vow will bind you ... to unremitting fatigue and to using all your strength and even your life in the service of the sick poor whom you will be obliged to receive, help and care for, day and night, with love, promptness, cheerfulness, and with the same honour and respect as you would render	By the Vow of Hospitality, the Little Sisters ... will use their strength and spend their lives, without fear of fatigue or discomfort, in the service of the aged and infirm poor whom they will be obliged to receive and feed according to their means, to help and nurse, day and night, striving to do

to Jesus Christ himself, since he it is whom we receive and care for in the persons of the poor, to whom in time past he said: He who receives you, receives me, and what you have done to the least of my little ones I regard as done to me.

this with the love and promptness, with the same honour and respect that they would show for Jesus Christ himself, since he it is in fact whom they receive and care for in the persons of the poor, of whom during his mortal life he said: He who receives you, receives me; and again: What you have done to the least of my little ones, I regard as done to me.

SOURCES FOR CHAPTER 21

MANUSCRIPT SOURCES

Archives des Petites Sœurs des Pauvres. Letters of the first Little Sisters of the Poor : Marie Jamet, Eulalie Jamet, Virginie Trédaniel.

Livres de fondation of the Angers and Rennes houses. Legal documents. A. Leroy, *Détails complémentaires* . . . op. cit.

PRINTED SOURCES CONTEMPORARY WITH JEANNE JUGAN

L. Aubineau, op. cit.

Ch. Dickens, 'The Little Sisters', in *Household Words, a weekly Journal conducted by Charles Dickens*, 14 February 1852.

Journal de Rennes, 8 June 1852.

Constitutions des Petites Sœurs des Pauvres, 1852.

Constitutions des Frères de Saint-Jean-de-Dieu, op. cit.

LATER STUDIES

A. Leroy, op. cit.

22

A STAGGERING HOAX

We saw how in 1843 the Abbé Le Pailleur quashed Jeanne's re-election and imposed his spiritual daughter Marie Jamet as Superior.

We have just seen how in 1852 he once and for all recalled the foundress to the mother-house when barely sixty years old, in full activity, her great prestige being likely to overshadow him.

We shall now see how he was to substitute himself for her as founder of the Congregation.

Already, in the years preceding, he had insinuated to people whom he knew, such as Monsieur Dupont, that he and his spiritual daughters had played the preponderant part in the origins of the Congregation; Monsieur Dupont, introduced by him to Jeanne Jugan, had gradually discovered the truth. We have witnessed a similar attempt in the case of Monsieur Chevremont, Secretary General of the Prefecture of Rennes. There too, the truth emerged on its own, and in the second edition of his book in 1873 Monsieur Chevremont was to make a point of insisting on the part played by Jeanne.

But from now on, a number of written documents were to present the legend and gradually get it accepted. The first is Léon Aubineau's extended article published in *L'Univers* in December 1851 and January 1852. In this first history of the Little Sisters of the Poor, Jeanne is presented merely as a collecting-sister; Monsieur Le Pailleur makes all the decisions; though a few passages lay stress on Jeanne's influence over her companions. These articles later appeared as a little book, reprinted some fifteen times between 1851 and 1884. And in these later editions, the passages stressing Jeanne's ascendancy were suppressed. In 1859, her name had practically disappeared; the attic in the rue du Centre had now become Fanchon's attic.

After 1877, the priest's part in the story was amplified: henceforth, he and he alone has the title of *founder*. Many details in it are pure romance.

Léon Aubineau also wrote the preface to Madame de La Corbinière's book in 1882. In this preface, he refers to his own book and observes,

> My little work once completed, I did not have the presumption to publish it without the founder's approval. The saints compel respect, and I should never have ventured to go against the *good Father*'s wishes. Besides, he alone has jurisdiction over, and is in a position to know everything about, his little family.

The *good Father* in fact said he was anxious 'not to wound the modesty' of those who had been both object and instrument in so many marvels. And made his own corrections to the text. Later on, he made corrections to Madame de La Corbinière's text too. The latter, though revering him, neatly allowed her amazement to show through (at various points in the book) at finding that things were not as she had first supposed.

We have seen how Louis Veuillot, after visiting Tours and conversing with Marie Jamet, gave an accurate account of the early days in *L'Univers*. Not long afterwards, however, he met the Abbé Le Pailleur. He too, in 1850, in *Les Libres Penseurs* (The Freethinkers)—second edition—radically reworks the text of his article in line with the legend crediting the said Abbé with the leading role.

This legend, deliberately created, also appears in official

documents. The first time is in the letter from the Bishop of Rennes to the Holy See, introducing the Congregation and soliciting pontifical approbation. In it, the date of the inception of the work has become 15 October 1840, whereas Jeanne had taken two poor women in nearly a year before. The Abbé is represented as the founder. Jeanne is only mentioned as one of 'four girls of humble condition'. The original draft of this letter has been found in the archives of the Bishop·ic of Rennes; it bears two corrections, considerably modifying the text and probably inserted by an accomplice after the Bishop had approved the draft. The adverb *praesertim* (in particular, especially), stressing Jeanne's role, has been struck out; and the word *fundatoris* has been added next to Le Pailleur's name.

Other falsifications were perpetrated: for instance, in the Diploma of Union granted by the Brothers of St John of God, Marie Jamet's name was substituted for that of Jeanne Jugan. When Jeanne died in 1879, the inscription put over her grave described her as the 'third Little Sister of the Poor'.

A tablet was placed on the *Maison de la Mansarde* (House of the Attic) at Saint-Servan in 1886,

> Here the Abbé Le Pailleur, founder of the Congregation of the Little Sisters of the Poor, began his hospitaller work by taking in a poor blind woman, whom he had caused, on 15 October 1840, his first two spiritual daughters, Marie Jamet and Virginie Trédaniel, to bring into the attic of this house, where Jeanne Jugan was living. To their number, the founder soon added Jeanne Jugan, who became the third Little Sister of the Poor, discharging the duty of collecting with admirable devotion.

The hoaxer was so skilful that the legend gradually came to be believed—not of course in circles where Jeanne had been known in the early days (the first witnesses gradually disappeared, unfortunately) but inside the Congregation itself, where from 1852 it replaced the true story in the training of the novices, not without causing some degree of astonishment, since a number of them had heard a different version of the facts in their own families.

Such behaviour leaves one confounded and can be explained only by a deep and subtle fault in Auguste Le Pailleur's psychological make-up. This systematic distortion of the truth is not necessarily incompatible with subjective sincerity.

As he grew older, his self-exaltation grew more and more pronounced. One Little Sister made the observation, 'It seems he has received too much adulation inside the Congregation and that this has turned his head. His journey through Spain was one continuous ovation, and when he came back, he was so infatuated with himself as to be unrecognisable. I saw this with my own eyes.'

Another one observed, 'The marks of respect which we were obliged to show him were very exaggerated; we even had to kiss his feet and ask his blessing if we met him when he was going for a walk.'

Good Madame de La Corbinière herself, her great admiration for the Abbé Le Pailleur notwithstanding, gave echo to the astonishment felt by the laity, 'What curtsyings! What prostrations!'

He wielded an absolute, centralised authority. Everything had to pass through his hands: admissions, foundations and so forth. He it was whom everyone had to approach, be the matter what it might.

Certain people's astonishment and even indignation were eventually taken note of in high places. A few years after Jeanne's death, an apostolic enquiry began. In 1890, Auguste Le Pailleur, already seventy-eight years old and having wielded his authority for more than forty years, was summoned to Rome; there he ended his days, in a convent.

Marie Jamet lived to see this conclusion, since she herself died in 1893. She was probably relieved by it. Her own good faith cannot be called into doubt; she must often have been torn between what she believed to be obedience, and her respect for the truth. A nun received the following avowal from her, 'I am not the first Little Sister, nor the foundress of the work. Jeanne Jugan was the first one and the foundress of the Little Sisters of the Poor.'

And the Abbé Leroy, who was chaplain at the mother-house, reported: 'I prepared Marie Jamet for death. This was what she said, "I am not the first one, but I was told to act as though I were." '

The same Abbé Leroy undertook, with great critical stringency, to conduct a historical investigation into the origins of the Congregation and to let in the light. Numerous facts and testimonies reveal the true succession of events in the early years. Outstanding among them is the *Memorial* sent to the Academy with a view to the Montyon Award: it was drawn up by eye-witnesses, and experts have established that it was written in Auguste Le Pailleur's hand: the latter thus giving himself the lie, by his own hand, in advance.

The Abbé Le Pailleur's behaviour has something odd about it, pointing to some kind of psychological disturbance. He was determined, even at the cost of falsifying the truth, to concentrate power and fame in his own person.

Even so, let us once again marvel at the way God entrusts his work to the frail and sinful hands of men, even respecting the very results of our shortcomings—not that this prevents him from eventually causing his grace to triumph when there is a humble heart to accept it and make it fruitful.

In this sense, Jeanne Jugan's long eclipse, her humble, loving prayer lasting for twenty-seven years, was perhaps—who knows?—the most productive period of her life.

SOURCES FOR CHAPTER 22

MANUSCRIPT SOURCES

Archives des Petites Sœurs des Pauvres. Testimony of Little Sisters of the Poor : Sœur Alexis de Sainte Thérèse, Sœur Esther de Saint Pacifique, Sœur Louise de l'Immaculée, Sœur Marie Hortense, Sœur Onésime de la Nativité. Note of Sœur Marie de la Croix (J. James), religious of the Saints Cœurs de Jésus et de Marie, of Paramé. Diploma of Union of Prayers, granted by the Brothers of St John of God. A. Helleu, *Notes et observations . . .* op. cit.

Archives de l'archevêché de Rennes. Letter of Mgr Brossais Saint-Marc to the Holy See, 12 September 1852.

PRINTED SOURCES CONTEMPORARY WITH JEANNE JUGAN

L. Aubineau, op. cit. See Appendices I and II.

Fr L. Veuillot, article quoted. See Appendices I and II.

LATER STUDIES

C. de La Corbinière, op. cit.

A. Leroy, op. cit.

23

SUMMARY OF TWELVE YEARS' ACTIVITY

(1840–52)

Much had taken place in the course of the twelve years 1840–52. In them, Jeanne had unfurled those hidden riches which, unknown to her, the Spirit of Jesus had prepared in her.

First, we saw her take a decisive step in giving up her bed to the aged Anne Chauvin; seized by the Spirit of Love, she was thenceforth to live by the light of love, drawing several noble-hearted girls along with her.

Then, in an act of trust, to give consistency to the work undertaken, she cuts her moorings and moves, with a larger number of dependants, into the *Big Downstairs*.

There, a new forward step towards self-identification with the poor: she begins to go begging in their place, on their behalf. An evangelical activity unalloyed. By begging, she probes people's consciences and at the same time manifests God's love for the world.

They then move into the Maison de la Croix, where there is more room, with the wider and better organised support of an entire town: it was as though many of her fellow-townspeople were falling into step with her on Charity's road.

Simultaneously, the association of the Servants of the Poor is beginning to take shape—but at the very moment when everything seems to be going ahead nicely, *her work is stolen from her:* resigning responsibility for it to someone else, she now experiences a new, more radical form of dispossession.

The humble maid receives an award from the French Academy: more than a financial boost, this provides the opportunity for making the labour undertaken known to a wide public. Jeanne does not confine herself to religious circles but enters, on an equal footing, into relationship with the organisations of this world, the whole of which is loved by God.

There are forsaken old people in other places; she takes those of Rennes to her heart and gives them a house. She has no resources: pure adventure of faith. She knows that the Father's love is at work and she goes forward with him.

After Rennes comes Dinan, where her ingenuity at organising mutual aid attracts attention. An English visitor is impressed by her intrepid trust.

She then travels from one town to another, tirelessly collecting, with that gift of hers for thawing hearts and drawing others into the sharing movement. Totally disinterested, she several times rescues the work no longer hers.

Then, at Tours, we see her being the missionary: she speaks *so simply and lovingly about Providence* that she it is who bestows the alms—alms of the Gospel.

Angers leaves us the impression of a happy epic, as the military band accompanies her certainty that she is co-operating with God's loving-kindness.

Meanwhile, in a matter of years, the original *little work* has expanded and its growth is getting faster. Postulants flow in, often called by Jeanne herself. Though not taking part in chapter-meetings, she sees her humble work take shape as a proper *Congregation*.

But she is about to experience a new deprivation as she gradually comes to realise that a legend is being created: while she is kept in the shades of the mother-house, some-

one else henceforth has himself called the *founder* of the
Little Sisters of the Poor.

In the course of this central period of her life, we see the
principal features of her *spirituality* growing clearer, that is
to say, her own, very individual way of living Christ's
Gospel.

The first thing we see is that she walks in the presence
of God; she performs all her actions with a lively awareness
of being dwelt in, loved and led by God. *Let us ring in God's
name*, she says. She refers everything to God, awaits everything from him: she speaks from experience about his *Providence*. For many people, this word, devalued by common
use, conjures up the picture of a useful God at the beck
and call of the devout. Not so for Jeanne: seized by Love,
living by Love, she knows his power and tenderness; she
opens herself to him by faith.

This faith in Love is expressed in continual, humble,
bold prayer: she never stops asking, *interceding* for the poor,
for benefactors, for the work which God has given her the
mission to perform. For her, St Joseph who cared for Mary
and Jesus is the sign of God's loving care for the aged poor.
For her, the evil of injustice and poverty is not a problem
for self-questioning, but a task to which she devotes herself,
co-operating with all her will with the love which God
lavishes on the world.

Prayer lays her open to love's impulsion, which she then
puts to work. Now love is primarily a sharing: letting
oneself be hurt by someone else's distress, putting oneself
at their side, living with, suffering with, begging with. She
naturalises herself as one of the poor; this is where love
works. And this process of sharing liberates the power of
love to change the world; by her astonishingly fruitful
activity, she contributes to changing the world. This is the
very mystery of *Mercy*.

She enters this mystery by *renunciation of self*, of all selfish ownership of herself or of her work. By means of human sorrows, the Spirit of God has actively stripped everything away, so that she may live, ever more radically, that mystery of death and resurrection inscribed in her by Baptism: not I but you, Lord; not my work but yours; not my immediate happiness, but the joy of the poor, who are You.

That is her *Poverty*: no need for her to wonder what norms she should adopt in order to live in Gospel poverty; the very motion of love strips all away and doubly so: total sharing with the poor whom she serves, and renunciation of any ownership in her work, in her success, in her poor. She takes no thought for what she herself shall eat; she knows that to whomsoever does the Gospel's work enough will be given and more. Before God and before her fellowmen, in her the Spirit creates a poor heart.

Since she is doing God's work, she has no need to bother about making methodical provision for the future; she goes ahead, from ricketty situations to dangerous adventures. *Dynamic of the provisional*: she begins with nothing, sets up house in an inconvenient corner, after a few months finds a better house, moves again; called by the expectant poor, she puts her faith in very young women, soon loaded down with responsibilities. She goes ahead in the *precariousness of hope*, sure of God. It is the haste of the Passover.

On man, on the world, she casts *a wide and trusting eye*; she knows that in this sinful world God is at work. In it she sees the poor, first of all—who are nearest to God, members of Christ in pre-eminent fashion—but she also sees all the possibilities for mutual aid and human solidarity ready to appear.

Attentive to God's work, she *lives in thanksgiving*. She marvels at the mutual aid of the poor, such as Isabelle Cœuru or sturdy Brisart; thanks to her, their names will live for ever. She gives thanks for the generosity of benefactors, however humble they may be; *she collects, praising*

God. She marvels at being loved so much and at seeing so much love passing through her to reach the poor and change the world.

Was it her lengthy meditating on the Heart of Christ from those early days in the Third Order that roused so dazzling and active a faith in Love?

PART III

RECOLLECTION

(1852–79)

24

LA PILETIÈRE

(1852–6)

At La Piletière, Jeanne Jugan was to bury herself in *little-ness*—a word she greatly loved.

The beggar-maid, that great walker of the roads of France, will not stir henceforth. Her new, entirely sedentary existence will first be led in this vast house, recently organised at the gates of Rennes. In one part of it is a home for more than a hundred old people (there will be three hundred of them in 1855), and in another part, the mother-house and novitiate, their numbers constantly rising. In February 1853, there were ninety religious in the house and sixty-four postulants. This was also the year of the first foundation in Belgium.

Sister Mary of the Cross—from now on, she was to have no other name, at least within the Congregation—was made responsible for directing the manual work of the postulants. One of them recalls the *kindness*, the *gentleness* with which she treated her young sisters; she had always loved, and won the love of, the young. In the strange circumstances which kept her immured in the mother-house, it must indeed have been a joy to her, to be involved in the youthful, fervent environment of these Little Sisters of the future. 'I never heard her utter the slightest word which might have led us to imagine that she had been the first Superior-General. She used to speak with great respect and deference of our first *good Mothers* (i.e. Superiors). She

155

was so little, so respectful in her relations with them.'

To begin with, perhaps she felt the better for the physical rest. For twelve years, she had been expending an immense amount of energy. And she seems to have been worried (as she had been long ago when living with Mademoiselle Lecoq) about *palpitations of the heart*, probably not severe, which often bothered her. She spoke about these, a little later, to Fr Ernest Lelièvre,[1] 'I've got something the matter with my heart. I can't last long. I am ready to go.' 'Don't worry,' he replied, 'you aren't going to die yet. I shouldn't be alarmed.' In point of fact, she had another twenty-five years of life ahead of her. It is a valuable piece of self-revelation, allowing us a glimpse of Jeanne in a moment of weakness and bringing her nearer to us.

But if Fr Lelièvre had not reported this memory many years afterwards, we should know nothing of this: strong in her weakness, Jeanne kept this sort of preoccupation to herself and never used to speak to her sisters about her health; she did not do so even when much later she experienced the infirmities of advanced old age. Discreet and cheerful, she was never one to dwell on her own troubles.

The Abbé Ernest Lelièvre (1826–89), whom we have just been quoting, had recently (in 1855), like Paul Gontard, given himself to the Little Sisters. Born of a family of industrialists of northern France, a doctor of law and theology, he not only brought his heart and intellect but his relatives, friends and a fortune as well. He was to give all unstintingly and play an important role in the expansion of the work, first in France, then in England, Scotland, Belgium, Malta, Spain, Ireland, the United States, North Africa and Italy. He died worn out at the age of sixty-three. He always held Sister Mary of the Cross in deep respect, recommending himself to her prayers before each

[1] The original spelling of this surname: *Le Liepvre*, was reassumed by the family in 1888, a year before Fr Ernest Lelièvre's death. The latter never adopted it.

of his journeys and keeping her up-to-date about his activities.

Jeanne was to see many Sisters much younger than herself die before her. Thus, she bade farewell, actually at La Piletière, to Virginie Trédaniel (12 August 1853), whom she had accepted long before as a very young girl at her guardian's request—not knowing at the time that she was to become one of the pillars of the *little family*.

Was it seeing this Sister depart at the age of thirty-two, or thinking back over the struggles and deprivations which she had endured since 1839, that one day made her say to the postulants, 'We have been grafted on to the Cross'?

She was not through with experiencing this. In December 1853, she was appointed a member of the General Council by decision of the Superiors. She was neither an assistant nor a councillor, but merely one of two Sisters who might be called to attend. In point of fact, throughout the next twenty-five years (she was to keep this title until 1878), only one instance of her attendance is recorded, in 1865—of which more later.

Another humiliation: after the Bishop of Rennes had approved the Congregation, she was not immediately allowed to pronounce perpetual vows, definitively admitting her to the religious state. Only Marie and Virginie (the Superior and the Assistant) made their profession on 8 December 1852. Jeanne was called to this two years later, with Madeleine Bourges and a number of others. On 8 December 1854—the self-same day as the proclamation of the dogma of the Immaculate Conception—Jeanne Jugan, then aged sixty-two, gave voice before the Church to the irrevocable gift which she had already been living for the previous fifteen years, not to mention her twenty-years' membership of the Third Order.

These troubles she endured in communion with the Cross of Christ. She knew that there is no other salvation than in the Paschal mystery of death and resurrection. And it is very likely that she perceived clearly enough the vital link existing between the death experienced in her heart throughout the years and the life welling up in her religious family.

On 12 September 1852, having just approved the Little Sisters' constitutions, the Bishop of Rennes had solicited recognition of the Congregation by the Holy See. An enquiry was opened under the chairmanship of Cardinal della Genga; bishops in whose dioceses the Little Sisters of the Poor had houses, had to express their views. At the outset, the Cardinal had frowned on seeing the role assigned to the *Fr Superior-General*. Eventually, on 9 July 1854, Pope Pius IX approved the Congregation of the Little Sisters of the Poor. The constitutions remained *ad experimentum*; more work would have to be done on them. The article concerning the *Fr Superior-General* was put aside for re-examination. Meanwhile, the Abbé Le Pailleur would remain in office as *promoter* of the Institute *ad bene-placitum Sanctae Sedis*. In January 1855, the article concerning the Fr Superior-General was suppressed, once and for all, by Rome, though the Little Sisters were never informed of this until 1 September 1867.

Since 2 December 1852, France had ceased to be a republic. The Prince-President had become the Emperor. Imperial approval could be useful to the Institute; it was applied for in 1855. To complete his investigation, the Prefect of Ille-et-Vilaine asked for a statement of 'the assets and liabilities' of the mother-house. Finding the reply unsatisfactory, he wrote again,

> To forestall any difficulty, I am obliged to return you the statement of the assets and liabilities of the community of the Little Sisters, begging you to take note that the assets indicate no resources for the feeding and maintenance of the Sisters or for the maintenance of buildings &c. The Council of State will

certainly wish to know whether the community possesses enough income to meet all obligatory expenses.

The perspicacious Prefect had put his finger on a grave deficiency: no income! no security other than prayer. It must be confessed they were about to ask the Council of State to pronounce on a matter hardly within its competence, a matter divine, neither more nor less!

The Secretary-General of the Congregation replied to this enquiry as follows,

> The assets of the Little Sisters show no income for the feeding and maintenance of the Sisters. They cannot show any, since there is none. The Sisters, in whichever establishment they are and depending to a greater or lesser extent on the number of old people there, are fed, as the latter are, on left-overs and the proceeds of collecting. As regards their clothing, this also comes through the generosity of others . . . The novitiate offers a few exceptions to the foregoing . . . All individuals admitted contribute towards their keep by bringing a dowry proportionate to their family circumstances.

(At this date there were thirty-six houses and about four thousand old people.)

Eventually approval was granted, thanks to the Empress Eugenie's personal intervention with the Minister of the Interior; Napoleon III's decree was dated 9 January 1856.

Did Jeanne know about this decree? There is no evidence that she did. Living with the postulants, she was not kept informed of the Congregation's affairs.

Even so, from the very modest position which she occupied, she must have seen many visitors, whether humble or illustrious, coming and going. Thus, for instance, in 1855, Louis Veuillot, who had written so eloquently about her in *L'Univers*, spent a few days at La Piletière with his friend Ernest Lelièvre. Prematurely widowed, Veuillot had just lost three of his young daughters in quick succession over a matter of months.

Sometimes Jeanne used to go into town to do some shopping or to pay a few visits. Thus it was that she renewed contact with the family of Monsieur René Guérin de La Grasserie who had given her such a kind reception in Rennes ten years before. Raoul de La Grasserie, then a little boy, later related how *dear Jeanne used to take him on her knee and smother him with loving kisses.* So, Sister Mary of the Cross went to see her old friends again. Now it happened that, staying with them at the time was a talented painter called Léon Brune; the two young daughters of the house were sitting for him. Discreetly, he made a sketch of the Sister; then painted her portrait from it. It is almost certain that she never saw it. The little picture[2] is of great value to us. Plainly, it does not prettify, does not disguise a certain coarseness of the features; but there is nothing commonplace in this firmly drawn face, with its straight nose, high cheek-bones, sunburnt complexion; the expression is grave, but there is a hint that the corners of the lips might easily rise in a friendly or bantering smile; the eyes, piercing beyond the visible, yet ready to meet an answering look—Jeanne seems to bear her sixty-three years with vigour.

She had struggled much, sympathised much, suffered much: *we have been grafted on to the Cross.* But, 'as though she could see the Invisible', she knew that Loving-kindness had already carried the day against Death.

---

[2] Léon Brune himself made two copies of this portrait; they have disappeared. The original was reverently preserved by the de La Grasserie family, who seem to have reproached the Congregation for having been unfaithful to the memory of the foundress. Relations were mended, however, with Mlle Renée de La Grasserie shortly before her death. She left the portrait to the Congregation (1972).

SOURCES FOR CHAPTER 24

MANUSCRIPT SOURCES

Archives des Petites Sœurs des Pauvres. Testimony of Little Sisters of the Poor : Sœur Scholastique reported by Sœur Germaine de Sainte Lucie, Sœur Adeline de Marie, Sœur Ignace de Sainte Marie, Sœur Saint Stanislas. Letters of Fr Lelièvre (4 May 1871; 1 September 1879). Correspondence with the public authorities and Imperial Decree of 9 January 1856.

Livre du conseil général and *livre de fondation* of the Rennes house.

Archives de l'archevêché de Rennes. Approbation of the Little Sisters of the Poor and correspondence with the Holy See.

Archives familiales de La Grasserie. Notes concerning relations with Jeanne Jugan.

STUDIES

L. Baunard, *Ernest Lelièvre et les fondations des Petites Sœurs des Pauvres d'après sa correspondance*, Paris, Poussielgue, 1904.

A. Leroy, op. cit.

25

LA TOUR SAINT-JOSEPH

(1856–64)

The flood of postulants kept growing. La Piletière in turn became too small. An even larger house had to be found, which this time would only contain the novitiate and mother-house.

A large estate came on the market in January 1856, called La Tour, at Saint-Pern, north of Rennes. It cost 212,000 francs, of which they only had 18,000. The Abbé Gontard sold one of his properties, and the Abbé Lelièvre, who had just arrived, paid off the balance. From those adaptations immediately necessary until the reconstruction of the principal dwelling-house had been completed, not excluding the building of the immense edifice destined to house up to six hundred novices and postulants, the work took more than twenty years. Every morning, groups of workmen on the roads throughout the area could be seen converging on the vast building-site.

The first three Little Sisters arrived on 1 April 1856; it was, as it happened, the feast of St Joseph, which had been transferred that year. Quite naturally, the property took the name La Tour Saint-Joseph. Twenty-seven novices arrived at the end of April; the postulants arrived in a body in June. Sister Mary of the Cross presumably came with one or other of these parties.

It seems, she was not given any specific duties: as occasion arose, she used to lend a hand to the Mother Mistress and the Sister Sub-mistress of the novitiate.

As we see her living there, hidden away, we shall glimpse something of the profound indwelling wisdom which she would henceforth be sharing with her young Sisters.

But first of all, what sort of events might be experienced at La Tour? What sort of things might set her mind thinking?

In the first place, there were the high days of the house itself.

On 25 July, Mgr Brossais Saint-Marc came to open the new building. He presided over an open-air profession of twenty-three novices. Many friends of the house were present at it, among them Monsieur and Madame de Falloux, close neighbours from now on. (Frédéric de Falloux had married Charlotte de Caradeuc de La Chalotais, and their Château de Caradeuc, at Bécherel, was only a mile and a quarter away from La Tour.) The newspapers covered the event. On 28 July, the *Journal de Rennes* reported: 'To witness the solemn inauguration of La Tour, henceforth to be used for training sisters for the poor, were all the Superiors of the forty houses where holy women, inspired by modest Jeanne Jugan's example, have erected charity into principle and action.'

Feast-days, ceremonies of clothing and profession, occurring year by year, brought groups of friends and relatives of the Sisters to La Tour. Various bishops known to the Congregation were called on to officiate. Thus, in 1857, Mgr Maupoint, a friend of long-standing who had just received episcopal consecration as Bishop of Réunion, came to lay the foundation stone of the new novitiate building.

On Wednesday 3 June 1857, La Tour received a visit from an American lady from Cincinnati, a great traveller, Mrs Sarah Peter. She was interested in the Little Sisters—she already hoped they would come to the United States—and wanted to get to know their mother-house. In a very enthusiastic letter, she relates how she was driven 'in their Breton carriage' from La Pilétière to La Tour. There she met Jeanne Jugan, 'the modest Breton servant-girl who started the Order'. She says, as had been explained to her, that Jeanne 'some few years ago resigned as head of the little Order and permitted Marie Jamet to become the Superior General.' And adds, admiringly, 'It is well worth the journey to become acquainted with Jeanne's modest, solid worth.' She notes the simplicity of the Sisters: 'a Polish countess and a Belgian marchioness' are lost among the others and indistinguishable from them. And what courage! 'No labour seems to frighten them. They are actually, with the assistance of workmen, building their stone house with their own hands. . . . How devoutly I pray they may come to us!'

There were days of sorrow too. In the autumn of the same year, four novices and a postulant died of typhoid fever. Two little ponds were drained, as supposedly responsible for the illness.

These events punctuated the henceforth regular, somewhat dull and monotonous life of Jeanne Jugan. In June 1858, she moved into the *bell-room* in the new novitiate building, and this she was to occupy for several years, sharing it with two novices.

What news penetrated the calm solitude of La Tour? Possibly she learnt in 1859 of the death of a poor parish priest near Lyons who for years had been attracting a continuous flood of penitents to his confessional-box . . . The world was changing. At the cost of immense labour, iron tracks now cut through the countryside; smoking steeds dashed along them, even faster than horses! The line from Rennes to Saint-Servan was opened in 1861; presumably Jeanne never took it.

There was also news of the Congregation itself: Sister Mary of the Cross was certainly thrilled to hear in 1863 that the first foundation had been made in Spain.

The following year, a family event took place, which may have made her smile: her brother Louis-Julien, who was a widower, got married again at the age of seventy-four, to the widow of a sailor who had lost his life in Newfoundland.

Jeanne had a message to hand on. Although it was modest and hidden, echoes of it still reach us from those Sisters, then novices or postulants, who had it impressed on them.

Thus, sharing her experience of humiliation and opposition with them, she would say, 'You have to be like a sack of wool, closing over the stone without a sound,' allowing ourselves to be fashioned by God, by making good use of events which can purge us and liberate us. One day, commenting on a reading, she said to some of the novices and postulants, 'You have just heard that you must do penance. What does that mean? How are you to do penance? For instance, two Little Sisters are out collecting; they have a lot to carry; it is raining, windy, they are wet &c. If they accept these discomforts bravely, submitting to the Will of God, they are doing penance!' Here we recognise the discreet and truly spiritual doctrine of the Eudist Third Order.

Is this another trace of the Third Order's influence? To the *Memorare*, the prayer so dear to St John Eudes, she would have them add, 'Grant, O Holy Virgin, that he who for our salvation was pleased to be born of you, may likewise through you receive our humble prayers' (a translation of the *Monstra te esse matrem*).

She was much concerned for those living about her; she could tell when they were unhappy or tired. One of them relates,

> When I was a brand-new postulant, Sister Mary of the Cross used to call me her *little acolyte*; she was thoroughly concerned about everything. One morning when it was time for exami-

nation of conscience, I was coming back from pulling up cabbage-stalks. Sister Mary of the Cross saw that I was dripping with sweat: she sent me off to change, so that I shouldn't catch cold.

Throughout these years we see her in high spirits; she loved singing (as in the days when she taught the catechism at Saint-Servan with dear old Mlle Lecoq!). Several people noted down memories like the following: on Christmas Day 1864, Sister Mary of the Cross was passing a group of postulants. Pleased to see her, they quickly gathered round her. She then started to sing, with them, *Jesus Christ is born today* . . . [1]

One day, great excitement, a famous hymn-writer paid a visit to La Tour. This was Fr Hermann, a Carmelite and man of God, who played a considerable role in his Order in France. The Sisters knew something of the inspiring story of this German Jew, Hermann Cohen (1821–71), who had been an infant prodigy as a pianist and a brilliant pupil of Liszt; later, in 1847, sharply jolted by God, he had been converted to the Christian faith, exercising great influence ever since. At La Tour, he met Sister Mary of the Cross among the novices; she recognised his name. 'Ah, Father,' she said, 'aren't you the one who sings so sweetly? . . . I wonder if you would care to sing these little novices a hymn?' 'Yes, Little Sister, though obedience gives me more satisfaction than singing.' So he obeyed. And sang, to everyone's delight, his hymn, *Peut-on vous voir, divine Eucharistie?* [2]

Thus Jeanne, *in littleness*, shared the life of the young; she loved them and they loved her. ·

Without wielding specific responsibilities, in the humble tasks of the community, she lived her faith and shared it. A loving, prayerful presence among those who had volunteered to follow the way of humble service which she herself had opened in 1839.

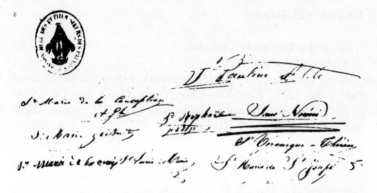

Signature of Sister Mary of the Cross (bottom left) on a letter to the Minister of Justice and Religious Affairs, 1865 (see Chapter 26).

SOURCES FOR CHAPTER 25

MANUSCRIPT SOURCES

Archives des Petites Sœurs des Pauvres. Testimony of Little Sisters of the Poor : Sœur Claire du Saint-Esprit reported by Sœur Alexis de Sainte Thérèse, Sœur Marie-Pierre reported by Sœur Adeline de Marie, Sœur Octavie Joseph reported by Sœur Martine de Sainte Thérèse, Sœur Saint Bruno reported by Sœur Aimée de Saint François, Sœur Ange de tous les Saints, Sœur Blanche de Sainte Marie, Sœur Paule-Thérèse.

Livres de fondation of the mother-house and Rennes house.

Archives municipales de Cancale. Records of civil registration.

PRINTED SOURCES CONTEMPORARY WITH JEANNE JUGAN

Journal de Rennes, 28 July 1856. *L'Auxiliaire Breton,* 29 July 1856.

---

[1] Actually, the popular French carol, *Il est né, le Divin Enfant.*

[2] 'Can we observe you, Eucharist Divine?'

LATER STUDIES

C. de La Corbinière, op. cit.

A. Leroy, op. cit.

A. S. McAllister, *In winter we flourish. Life and letters of Sarah Peter (1800–1877)*, New York, Longmans, Green and Co, 1939.

Dictionnaire de spiritualité (Beauchesne), art. 'Hermann' (Hermann Cohen, dit le P. Hermann).

26

NO REGULAR INCOME!

(1865)

Sister Mary of the Cross, 'upright, supporting herself with a big walking-stick . . . walked the fields and woods of La Tour Saint-Joseph giving thanks to God . . . and whenever she saw old friends who knew something of the beginnings of the work . . . she would sing her Magnificat. [She] was truly eloquent in her simplicity.' Thus Léon Aubineau described her, having presumably seen her at his sister-in-law's profession on 29 September 1865.

She was then seventy-three and still as tall and thin as ever.

She was carefully excluded from any position of responsibility; she was never summoned to attend the General Council, of which she had nominally been a member for the previous twelve years.

Once, however, she did take part in the deliberations of the Council of her Congregation. Her signature attests it.

This was on 19 June 1865. An important problem had to be discussed, one affecting the very essence of the vocation of a Little Sister of the Poor. It concerned the observance of poverty, and exclusive reliance on God's providence. Up till then, they had always wanted to be entirely dependent on charity, without relying on any investment, without counting on any regular income. No regulation specifically laid this down but it was actually implicit in the collecting instituted by Jeanne: to become poor with the poor and with them commit oneself totally to God. Such was the spirit.

True, houses had been acquired. Jeanne herself had actively taken part in purchasing the Maison de la Croix at Saint-Servan and the Capuchin Convent in Dinan; she had contributed to later purchases by her collecting. These houses constituted 'the patrimony of the poor'.

In the early days, a few regular sources of income and endowments had certainly been accepted—for such occasionally was the form taken by the charity on which they wished to depend. In 1851, the house at Saint-Servan could count on an income of 2,300 francs (in a budget exceeding 12,000 francs). The same year, the house in Dinan received a large legacy of 10,000 francs, to be invested 'in Government stock', so as to constitute a 'perpetual donation'; the money, handed over to and invested by the Municipality, brought in 500 francs a year.[1] But these investments had never represented more than a small fraction of the income needed and had always apparently been regarded as exceptional cases. In 1855, in answer to an enquiry from the Prefect of Ille-et-Vilaine as regards the regular income of the Congregation, it had still been accurate to say that there was none and that everything came from collecting. That was the principle of the thing.

Ten years, however, had now gone by; the time was now 1865. A legacy of 4,000 francs, after others, had been made to the Congregation. And again the question arose: should it be accepted or refused? At the time, the Comte de Bertou, a friend of the Little Sisters, was helping them administer their finances. He it was who sounded the alarm. 'If you will allow me to give my humble opinion,' he wrote, 'you should accept it only if authorised to forgo the interest and

---

[1] The money was handed over to the Municipality because the Congregation, as yet having no civil identity, was not capable of ownership. As already noted, recognition was granted by imperial authority in 1856.

to use the capital sum to pay for your house [in Paris]. You should own only the houses you live in, and otherwise live on daily charity. If the Little Sisters were thought to have investments, they would lose their right to that charity which kept the Israelites alive in the wilderness, and if once they were to start storing up manna, the manna would go bad in their hands, as happened long ago to God's people.'

We shall get a clearer idea about the implications of this hesitancy about economic security, if we consider it in its historical context: the great upsurge of modern capitalism in France. In those years of the Second Empire, there was a kind of febrile ebullience over money and business. A whole literature was devoted to it: the Comtesse de Ségur herself wrote *La Fortune de Gaspar*! The great banks were founded or developing: The Crédit Lyonnais came into existence in 1863, the Société Générale in 1864. In 1865 a law introduced the use of the cheque into France. Businesses were being set up, joint-stock companies floated, powerful financial groups formed. Colossal fortunes were being made for all to see. Between 1850 and 1869, the Paris Bourse tripled the number of shares quoted. 'The Bourse represents for this generation what the cathedrals represented for the Middle Ages' (Alexandre Dumas, *fils*).

Now, precisely at this time, in 1865, the Little Sisters of the Poor were to take and inform the public authorities of the solemn decision not to accept any sort of regular income.

They had asked several bishops for their opinions; then the General Council met.

And it was to this meeting that, absolutely without precedent, Sister Mary of the Cross was summoned. Taken by surprise, she seems at first to have excused herself from attending: 'I am only a poor ignorant woman; what can I contribute?' But they insisted. 'Since you wish it, I shall obey.' And she gave her opinion, firmly. The right thing, she said, was to go on refusing any regular income and rely on charity. And that was the view which eventually prevailed.

All the houses were notified forthwith. The circular states that 'the Congregation cannot own investments or any regular income of a permanent sort, and that consequently we shall refuse any legacy or gift consisting of investments or entailing the endowment of beds or Masses or any other kind of permanent obligation.' The Sisters of the Poor resolved to go on living the *dynamic of the provisional*, which they had chosen from the outset.

Most important, the Council drew up a letter to be sent to the Minister of Justice and Religious Affairs, informing him of this decision. And it is this very letter which bears the signature of Sister Mary of the Cross.[2] The government was to give its official agreement in January 1866, taking note, by virtue of the same, of their refusal of the legacy over which the question had arisen.

Jeanne was unquestionably happy about this decision. In it, she recognised an answer to her continual prayer. A little later, she was still encouraging the novices and postulants to pray 'that there would be no giving in to the entreaties of those who wanted to give us stocks and shares.'

Ceaselessly in her prayers she kept watch over the Congregation to which she had given birth—and most particularly over this family's loyalty to its special vocation of poverty and faith. And surely it was her assiduous prayer, her lengthy vigil, her indefectible waiting, which allowed the Spirit of Christ, once the moment came, to utter the decisive words through her and keep the Little Sisters of the Poor constant to their original spirituality.

[2] The signature is reproduced on page 167.

SOURCES FOR CHAPTER 26

MANUSCRIPT SOURCES

Archives des Petites Sœurs des Pauvres. Testimony of Little Sisters of the Poor : Sœur Saint Albert, Sœur Véronique de Saint Joseph. Letter to the Garde des Sceaux (Minister of Justice), 19 June 1865, and Imperial Decree, 9 January 1856. Bequests of Néel de la Vigne and Borgnis-Gallanty. Note of Comte de Bertou.

Livres de fondation of the Saint-Servan and Dinan houses.

Archives municipales de Saint-Servan. Deliberations of the Municipal Council (1845). Mayor's correspondence (1845–54).

PRINTED SOURCES CONTEMPORARY WITH JEANNE JUGAN

J. Lesage, *Mémoires* . . . op. cit.

LATER STUDIES

C. de La Corbinière, op. cit., with preface by L. Aubineau.

A. Leroy, op. cit.

A. Plessis, *De la fête impériale au Mur des Fédérés,* Paris, Seuil, 1872.

27

IN THE BELL-ROOM

(1866–9)

Jeanne, though unknown within her community, was an illustrious person in many people's eyes.

At Saint-Servan, which she had left a long while previously, she had not been forgotten: the people of Saint-Servan were proud of her. On 28 May 1866, the Municipal Council decided to rename the street running past the Maison de la Croix in her honour; it was no longer to be the *rue Vigne-au-Chapt* but the *rue Jeanne Jugan*. Jeanne heard the news and was upset by it. One day, the Abbé Collet, parish priest of Saint-Servan, came to see her. She begged him to intervene, so that the street would not go on being called after her; it ought to be called the *rue de la Providence*, she said. And indeed, within the Congregation, the secretariat received instructions—though not so as to please her on this point—to ignore the change and address the letters as before to the *rue Vigne-au-Chapt*.

Even at Saint-Pern, a great many people revered her and attached great value to her prayers. She lived by faith, offering continual supplication to God. Thus, she prayed, and caused others to pray, for the workmen building the house and chapel, 'that no accident should befall them'. Now, on 3 January 1867, in an attempt to clear the snow which was hindering work on the chapel belfry, a young workman slipped and had a terrible fall: he bounced off a lower roof and fell into a heap of sand—before his own father's very eyes. But the only ill-effects he sustained were two months in bed and a slight deafness in one ear. Two other similar incidents are on record.[1] The son of one of these lucky men became a priest; he recorded this memory: 'I can still hear my mother saying to me, "It's a miracle! It's due to the foundress of the Little Sisters of the Poor!"'

The following year, Madame Tostivint, the mother of a family, went into the chapel with her children. She was carrying one of them, although he was four or five years old; he had never walked. Hoping and asking for him to be cured, she prayed in front of the altar of St Pacificus (a Roman martyr whose relics had been presented to La Tour four years before, thanks to the Superior-General of the Brothers of St John of God). She then came out, still carrying the child. She met Jeanne. The latter apparently took him in her arms for a moment, then put him down on the ground, saying, 'Little one, what a weight you are!' Be that as it may, she let him hold her walking-stick and he began walking of his own accord, under his astonished mother's eyes, 'Little John's walking! He's walking with Jeanne Jugan's stick!'

These facts show what veneration, what faith the local people had in Jeanne.

The Congregation continued its rapid growth. In March 1867 there were a hundred postulants at La Tour. The same year, the hundredth house was opened—in Toulon. In 1868, foundations began in North Africa, Ireland and America. (In the last two countries, they were in large measure the work of Fr Lelièvre.) On 8 October 1868, eleven years after Mrs Peter's visit, the first Little Sisters left for the United States; it was an important event at La Tour—and an event in Jeanne's heart. In 1869 came the first foundation in Italy.

[1] See *Positio super Virtutibus*, p. 384.

Jeanne held each of these advances in her continual supplication, ever mingled with thanksgiving. In March 1868, Eulalie Jamet wrote from Madrid, 'Thank Sister Mary of the Cross for the novenas she makes. I beg her to continue.'

Yes, Jeanne kept vigil before God in uninterrupted prayer. She interceded especially for the postulants whom she saw arriving in such numbers at La Tour and whose life she shared.

She was anxious to help them become true *sisters* to the poor, thoroughly supple in God's hand, transparent to the Love who wished, through them, to give himself to the poor.

Always so straight and upright of bearing herself, Jeanne wished her young sisters to express their deeply spiritual nature in their own bearing and behaviour. Sometimes, it might be, they were rather excitable or thoughtless. Others retained more or less affected ways. Sister Mary of the Cross would correct them gently, and sometimes firmly. One day, noticing a young Sister who had rather worldly manners, she said to a novice, 'Show this little one how a Little Sister ought to walk and behave when out collecting!' In a corridor, she encountered Sister Claire who was running at top speed; she stopped her, 'You're leaving someone behind, Little Sister!' Intrigued, Sister Claire turned round: 'Excuse me, *my good Little Sister*, but I can't see anyone.' 'Yes, you are! You're leaving God behind! He is letting you run on ahead, for Our Lord never used go to so fast and was never in a hurry like you are.' Note the Gospel reference to the Lord Jesus. For her, this was a kind of reflex action, actually part of herself.

Another time, she said to a young Sister (who was later put in charge of training), 'If you want your Little Sisters to be more composed . . . make them reflect that, being brides of Our Lord, they are always with him. He doesn't

care for noise. Thinking that Our Lord is near them will
do more good than the stiffest of lectures.'

Some of her interventions—very exceptionally—seem to
have been less fortunate. It happened, they say, that to test
a novice's faith and obedience, she sent her to water a dead
tree—which rather irritated Sister Paule, who was in
charge of the gardening. In fact, it seems, Jeanne soon gave
up this sort of practice, current in novitiates of the day
though hardly in keeping with her own humane, direct,
free personality.

Be that as it may, she believed that the postulants, by
accepting advice and practical illustrations, allowed God
himself to fashion them into being more supple to serve
him. One Sister relates that one day Sister Mary of the
Cross called her over to an open window from which they
could see the workmen cutting blocks of stone for the chapel
(begun in 1861). She said to her, 'Look at those workmen
cutting the white stone for the chapel, and how fine they
make the stone look. You must let Our Lord cut you like
that!' Another day, walking past a rose bush, she said to
one of the novices, 'You see these rose bushes, they're little
wild ones. And you are a little wild rose too. But if you let
yourself be properly trained, you will turn into a beautiful
rose formed by God's own love. But you must allow yourself to be humbled. Instead of going down into yourself, go
up towards God!'

During the year 1869, it seems that Sister Mary of the
Cross, though by now very old, was temporarily put in
charge of the postulants. She was the life and soul of recreation periods. During the day, she was habitually to be
found in the sewing-room, knitting black woollen stockings;
but she was already beginning to suffer with her eyes and
could not concentrate for long at a time. The memory of
her kindness has been preserved. 'She was a kind little
mother to us and we loved her dearly.' When she passed

a group of them, she always had a friendly word or two to say. If they were cold, Jeanne would take them out into the garden to warm their feet up. To keep time as they walked, she used to make them repeat a sort of counting-rhyme, while she marked time with her stick:

> One, two, three,
> step out today,
> step out tomorrow,
> step out every day
> and a long way you'll go!

She loved laughing and making others laugh. 'What is your name, Little Sister?' 'Sister Pascaline.' 'The dear old people in the houses will call you Sister Percaline!'[2] And everyone roared with laughter.

In the course of conversation, she often mentioned the aged. And then a thrill would run through her very being; they were her life. 'We are blessed', she would say in enthusiastic tones, 'to be a *little sister of the poor* [the italicised words should be given their full weight]. Making the poor happy is everything ... never causing suffering to anyone old and poor. We must *spoil* them all we can.'

She often insisted on the duty of praying for benefactors: it should be real, personal, responsible prayer. 'You are to say the rosary for our benefactors. How grateful we ought to be to them. What could we do for our dear old people without them? We must pray, and pray hard!'

Like St Dominic, like the Curé d'Ars, 'she *groaned* over the loss of souls—especially the souls of the aged.' Often, very often, she would say to the novices and postulants, 'Knock, knock at Heaven's gate for souls!' Or again, she would mention somebody in particular, 'Pray that such-

---

[2] Glazed cotton material used for lining clothes.

and-such a soul may be converted!' She had, we are told,
'a special weakness for prisoners and those under sentence
of death'.

Before all else, she set the Eucharist at the heart of her
life—and the Eucharist, to her mind, was universal. She
encouraged the Sisters to recite the Lord's Prayer at the
same time as the priest (the time had not yet come for
saying it all together). 'She would explain to them about
the great efficacy of those petitions when united to those of
Our Lord, represented by the priest.' And at night, when
she could not sleep, she would unite herself to the Masses
being celebrated in distant lands.

It seems that her spiritual life was very lively, very sustained, but also very simple and fairly stark; she lived all
things in a spontaneous, generally uncomplicated, familiarity with God, in connivance with him, as it were. The vital
bond linking her to him passed by way of poverty; the
poverty of self-renunciation committed her entirely to him
in whom she put her trust—and material poverty, firmly
wished for her spiritual family, made her await her suste-
nance from the very Love which had raised her up and
offered itself through her to be shared by the aged poor.

SOURCES FOR CHAPTER 27

MANUSCRIPT SOURCES

Archives des Petites Sœurs des Pauvres. Letters and fragments of the
first Little Sisters of the Poor : Marie Jamet, Eulalie Jamet.
    Testimony of Little Sisters of the Poor : Sœur Claire du
Saint Esprit reported by Sœur Alexis de Sainte Thérèse, Sœur
Epiphane Joseph reported by Sœur Marie de Saint Martin, Sœur
Gabrielle Thérèse reported by Sœur Bernardine de l'Epiphanie,

Sœur Thérèse de la Conception reported by Sœur Louise de l'Immaculée, Sœur Ursule reported by Sœur Delphine de Saint Jean, Sœur Alexis de Sainte Thérèse, Sœur Blanche de la Conception, Sœur Cécile de la Nativité, Sœur Céline de l'Ascension, Sœur Eléonore de Saint Paul, Sœur Ludivine de la Croix, Sœur Maria de Saint Maurice, Sœur Marie Lambertine, Sœur Marie Octavie, Sœur Michel Arsène, Sœur Pascaline, Sœur Saint Albert, Sœur Sainte Eusébie, Sœur Saint Michel, Sœur Siméone Joseph, Sœur Thérèse Augustine, Sœur Virginie Marie.

Other testimony : Mgr Collet, 6 December 1895, Canon Durand, 14 August 1961, Marie-François Tostivint, 5 April 1935, Canon Désiré Tostivint, 13 October 1923.

Livre de fondation of the mother-house. Letters of Fr Lelièvre.

Archives municipales de Saint-Servan. Deliberations of the Municipal Council.

LATER STUDIES

L. Baunard, op. cit.

28

THE INFIRMARY ROOM
(1870–2)

In 1870, Jeanne had for some time been living in *the infirm-ary room*, which she was to occupy until her death. It is a large room, in the middle of the main block of the novitiate, on the first floor; you only need to cross the corridor to be in the tribune of the chapel. There she lived with three other Sisters. She took her meals there, alone, which saved her from having to go downstairs, since by then she found it harder to walk owing to an ulcer on her leg. A novice had the duty of looking after her, of keeping the room clean and of bringing her her meals.

A photograph was taken of Jeanne at about this time:[1] tall, straight, her head tilted back a little and the eyelids lowered owing to the infirmity which made it more and

[1] This unique photograph of Jeanne bears the trade-name Gilbert, Senior, painter and photographer, 6 *bis*, rue de Bel-Air, Rennes. The theory has been advanced that it was taken after Jeanne's death, on the strength of the somewhat peculiar look given her by her half-closed eyes. It seems, however, that it does in fact date from the years 1870–1. For the Rennes directory (*Almanach des Adresses*) of 1872 has the entry, 'Le Michel, successor to Gilbert, 6 *bis*, rue de Bel-Air, Rennes'. And a photograph of the Mother Superior-General has been found, taken before 21 April 1872, signed: Le Michel, successor to Gilbert. Jeanne's photograph must, therefore, have been taken earlier, when Gilbert was still in business.

This photograph inspired the Brussels painter, Ernest Wante (who never had the opportunity of seeing Léon Brune's picture, since the Congregation did not then know of its existence), when he painted the large portrait of Jeanne in 1935, presented to the Mayor's office at Saint-Servan in 1960.

Similarly, Fr Marie-Bernard of the Soligny Trappists worked from an enlargement of this photograph when making a statue (1954) and sundry medallions (1959–64).

more difficult for her to open her eyes wide.

She remained particularly attached to the postulants, of whom by then there were more than a hundred. She attended the sewing-room, enlivened their recreation periods. She was still full of life.

On these Little Sisters—her *Benjamins* as she called them—she bestowed a loving attention proportionate to each, keenly concerned for their balance and well-being. If she noticed a sad, tense face, she would enquire gently, advise a little walk . . . In the garden, if she met a young Sister carrying too heavy a load or pushing an overloaded barrow, specially if she happened to be a town-bred girl who was not used to such work, she would discreetly have a word with the Sister-in-charge. One summer, the Little Sister who looked after her was working on the threshing-machine in the sun and dust; she sent for her: 'It's very hot; you're tired; you must have a rest. Sit down and do some sewing. I'll fetch you all the things you need.' Every day, two Little Sisters used to go and fetch the letters from the post office at Bécherel; if it was raining, Sister Mary of the Cross used to make sure that they had not got wet: 'Look, little ones, you must be absolutely straightforward with your Superiors, and not catch cold through your own fault, for your health is not your own. It belongs to God, who wants to employ you with the poor.'

On the same theme, she laughingly related one of her memories from the days of her first collecting-rounds.

One day I was out collecting, I had walked a long way already, when someone gave me a lovely rabbit. Having thanked them very much and put the rabbit in my basket, I went on. The further I went, the heavier that rabbit became. And I began to think how happy the little creature would be to run wherever it pleased, and what a relief it would be for me not to have to carry it . . . I raised the lid of the basket, telling myself that a Little Sister's health was worth more than a rabbit!

Façade of the manor-house of La Tour at Saint-Pern, when the mother-house and novitiate were installed there in 1856 (see Chapter 25)

Scene from hospitaller life in London, by James Collinson (for explanation, see Appendix IV)

This, the only photo preserved of Sister Mary of the Cross, apparently dates from 1870–1. Jeanne was nearly eighty (see Chapter 28)— *Photo Gilbert Senr, reproduced by A. Maurice*

Tribune of the chapel at La Tour Saint-Joseph, where Sister Mary of the Cross loved to spend hours in prayer during the last ten years of her life (see Chapters 27 and 28) —*Photo T. Piccari*

She showed her concern for the more timid ones who had difficulty in expressing themselves. If, in the course of conversation, a somewhat quicker-witted Little Sister interrupted another one, she would intervene in such a way as to allow the latter to finish what she had started to say: 'Our Little Sister hasn't quite finished . . .'[2]

She also showed concern over the lives of men, over events in the world and in the Church. She very much liked the Fathers to come and see her when they returned from their travels, and tell her what they had seen and what they had done. She was interested in everything.

She was much concerned about the serious events of 1869–71, first the Vatican Council, then the Franco-Prussian War which brought it to a halt. The war and ensuing occupation of France, in any case, had repercussions on the life of the novitiate for several months. From America, Fr Lelièvre echoed the news which had reached him from La Tour. It 'is scarcely more comforting than the rest: all the novices scattered, building suspended, only a handful of postulants wandering about in that huge house, dormitories awaiting the wounded, and poverty almost as bad as that in the countries already laid waste by the war, in a word—desolation.'

With the Catholics of her day, Jeanne was distressed to see the Pope deprived of his States by the powers. 'From the fervent prayers which she made us say each day,' one Little Sister relates, 'I came to grasp what a deep attachment she felt for Holy Church and the Sovereign Pontiff Pius IX.' She urged the young to pray to God for all men; all human distress was to be brought before the Lord.

Then more peaceful times returned and the life of the house resumed its course. When the weather was fine, stick in hand and leaning on a novice's arm, Sister Mary of the

---

[2] This detail dates from slightly later (about 1879).

Cross liked to range the rolling countryside of the park, the high woods which had provided the beams for the house, the copses springing up sturdily after being cut, the steep slopes, the ponds with their glittering reflections and the plopping of frogs, the granite quarries with their precipitous sides. From time to time, she would run into a group from the novitiate; if she was not too tired, she would wave her stick, and the novices or postulants would come joyfully running. She would pass the time of day with them, share a thought with them, then, using her stick again, signal to them to be off. And the sparrows would take flight.

A lifetime's experience was distilled into these brief conversations.

Sometimes, when she was walking through the fields or gardens, a flower would arouse her admiration. She would say to her young companion, 'Do you know who made this?' 'God did,' the Little Sister would reply. Then Jeanne would look her in the eye and say with a look of intense gratitude, 'Our Bridegroom did!' This was one of the themes on which she meditated at the time. One winter, she stood at the window with a postulant to gaze at the snow mantling the ground, the roofs, the trees in the garden. 'Look, how lovely it is! My Bridegroom has done all this!' Then, turning to the young Sister, 'And he will be yours too!'

'She often used to speak to us', says one Little Sister, 'about the holy presence of God—in us, in the tabernacle and in the poor. And she often reminded us to love them dearly and always to look on them as the suffering members of Our Lord.' Note the unitary quality of her faith, recognising the same presence *in us, in the tabernacle and in the poor.* (St John Eudes, whose disciple she was, would frequently say that the poor were 'the sacraments of the Saviour'. He saw Christ present in them 'almost as in the elements of the Eucharist'.[3])

A number of Sisters were struck by her radiantly joyful bearing and loving concentration when she made the sign of the cross or approached the Sacrament of Holy Communion. To see her 'made one long to love the Eucharist as she loved it.' 'How we loved to watch this dear Little Sister . . . respectfully make her lovely sign of the cross!'

She, however, preferred the path of discretion in the way she prayed. After reciting a few prayers with the novices, 'she often used to insist that, later on, we should be careful not to say too many of these prayers of devotion. "You will weary your old folk," she would say, "they will get bored and go off for a smoke . . . even during the rosary!" '

She was always reverting to the aged. She would often tell the novices and postulants about her experiences in serving them. To one of these, she passed on some traditional recipes for making herbal drinks and cataplasms. She added, 'The aged are grateful for small attentions, and these are a way of winning them for God.'

One day, a novice was doing housework in the room over Jeanne's bedroom. Jeanne had her called, 'Dear child, when you are doing housework, especially near the sick, you must take care not to be noisy with things, use them cautiously, do not clack your heels as you walk . . . It is very tiring for the sick. Be very quiet!'[4]

When she spoke of the poor, 'her heart used to overflow.' 'Dear children,' she would say, 'let us love God dearly and the poor in him.' Or again, 'With the eye of faith, we must see Jesus in our old people—for they are God's mouthpiece.'

She would often come into the sewing-room and go from table to table. Sometimes she would pause and chat a little

---

[3] P. Herambourg, *Saint Jean Eudes . . . Ses vertus*, published by D. Boulay, Paris, 1927, p. 202.
[4] This detail dates from slightly later (about 1874).

longer. One day, for instance, she was thinking about the
Holy Family at Nazareth,

> Think, little ones, how dearly all three of them loved one
> another! How happy they looked! How kindly, how gently,
> they spoke to one another! In our little family, we must do
> the same. . . . The Blessed Virgin was poor too; she did as the
> poor do, she never wasted her time, for the poor cannot afford
> to sit idle, and in this we should imitate the Holy Family.
>   Little ones, you must always be cheerful. Our little old
> people do not like long faces.

That sum of wisdom, slowly acquired, or rather knit
together in her by the Spirit of Jesus through the long years
as he was showing her how best to serve the poor, Jeanne
now shared with her young Sisters.

And, to close this period, here is a rather dramatic incident. We are now in July 1872 at the start of a General
Chapter of the Congregation. Some novices are working in
the garden. Sister Mary of the Cross is saying her rosary
in the alleys. Not far away, some workmen are working in
the farm buildings. Suddenly there is a commotion; shouts
and bellowings ring out. 'Get out of the way, get out of the
way!' An enraged bull has escaped from the cattle-shed
and the workmen have not been able to control it. It is
wrecking everything in its path. 'Little ones, lie on the
ground!' Jeanne shouts. She stays on her feet and raises
her little stick: 'Stop, I command you!' The brute calms
down and walks harmlessly by the Little Sisters; the workmen recover control of it. And Sister Mary of the Cross
goes silently on with her rosary.

Attentive. Attentive to those around her, attentive to the
life of the world, attentive to God so lovingly sought—but
it was the same attentiveness, whether directed towards
God or towards others, since 'he dwells in them and they
in him.' She rested a prayerful gaze on each individual,

attentive to the Poor Man. Jeanne Jugan's silence was the silence of listening, of receiving, of loving attentiveness.

SOURCES FOR CHAPTER 28

MANUSCRIPT SOURCES

Archives des Petites Sœurs des Pauvres. Testimony of Little Sisters of the Poor : Sœur Alexis de Sainte Thérèse, Sœur Alphonse de la Nativité, Sœur Anaïs Joseph, Sœur Angélique de Saint Paul, Sœur Auguste Alexis, Sœur Catherine de tous les Saints, Sœur Clémentine Joseph, Sœur Denise de Saint Joseph, Sœur Ignace de Sainte Marie, Sœur Luce de Saint Louis, Sœur Marie Octavie, Sœur Noël Joséphine, Sœur Prosper de Saint Joseph, Sœur Sidonie de Sainte Anne, Sœur Sophie de Sainte Marie, Sœur Saint Albert, Sœur Sainte Amélie, Sœur Saint Théotime.

Letters of Fr Lelièvre. Correspondence of Fr Marie-Bernard, Soligny Trappist. Photograph by Gilbert.

29

'VERY LITTLE BEFORE GOD'

(1873–5)

1873. At Alençon a little girl is born who will later be known as Thérèse Martin. At La Tour Saint-Joseph, old Little Sister Mary of the Cross falls sick. She spent several weeks in bed. Then she got better, but at eighty-one did not recover quite the vigour of earlier days. Thenceforth her presence was no longer required in the sewing-room, and a novice was assigned to accompany her on her walks. Inside the house, she could still walk about on her own but she needed someone to help her up the stairs. She would wait until a Little Sister happened to come along and then ask her to support her. Once up, she would thank her graciously and promise to pray to the Virgin for her.

Standing up, she retained her proud carriage. A young English woman saw her at this period,

> walking with so firm a step, leaning upon the arm of a young Little Sister with one hand and upon a stout walking-stick with the other, so erect and alert, that it seemed to us as if she scarcely needed any support, as she took a few turns with us in the wide alleys of the garden . . . That which struck us most about her, was the exceeding sweetness of her smile, which lit up her face as it rested upon the person to whom she was speaking . . . When we bade her farewell and asked her to pray for our little girl too young to come with us, she took from her pocket a little round wooden case, containing a statue of St Joseph (every Little Sister carries a figure of St

Joseph the Provider in her pocket) and said, 'Give this to your little child as a souvenir of Sister Mary of the Cross.'[1]

When a small group of Sisters came to visit her, she would sometimes suggest a short spiritual reading. She would have a page read aloud from *The Man of Prayer*[2] by her beloved Fr Nouet, a book which had been her companion for many years and to which she constantly returned. She liked to add her own little personal commentary on the reading, and this often turned on the Lord Jesus's kindness, his gentleness, his compassion for all human ills. One day, during a reading, there had been something about *holy tears*. She told the reader to shut the book and said to the Sisters,

> Some of you may find this hard to understand and say, 'I can't weep . . . And I wouldn't want to be weeping all the time.' Don't you worry your heads over *holy tears*. There's no need to get your eyes wet shedding any! But willingly making a sacrifice, peaceably accepting a rebuke—this counts as holy tears. I'm sure you've wept like this several times today already.

How well this illustrates her smiling sense of humour, as well as the very interior character of her spiritual way!

Another time, the reading mentioned a hawk swooping down on a helpless little bird. Jeanne's commentary, 'We should have no more strength against temptation than this

[1] Little Violet Ram became a Religious of the Sacred Heart. The statuette was often lent to the Little Sisters on their collecting rounds in London, especially when times were hard. Eventually it was given to Sister Agnès Onésime and then returned by her to the mother-house.
[2] *L'Homme d'Oraison* by Jacques Nouet (1605–80), a Jesuit known for his controversies with the Jansenists and Protestants, as also for his spiritual writings. His works were reprinted in 1837 in twenty-seven little volumes. The collection is entitled *L'Homme d'Oraison*, but the title applies more particularly to a treatise on prayer: *L'Homme d'Oraison, sa conduite dans les voies de Dieu* (The Man of Prayer, his conduct in the ways of God). The other volumes contain meditations, spiritual readings, retreats.

little bird had to resist the hawk, were God not to give us his help. We must be convinced of this when we ask him for it; and that should increase our trust, since by God's power we can triumph.'

On 29 April 1874, the postulants were joined by someone no longer a young woman. She was Mme Féburier, whose husband, a member of the Society of St Vincent de Paul in Paris, had largely paid for the building of the chapel. He had died in 1873 and been buried in the crypt. His widow then decided to join the Little Sisters. 'There's someone', Jeanne used to say, 'who knows how to give to God! She was educated at the Visitation. she used to be a great lady, and now she's become a Little Sister of the Poor!' One day, Mme Féburier offered Jeanne her arm to take her upstairs. Sister Mary of the Cross, ever *little*, later was to say, 'If I hadn't been afraid of hurting her feelings, I should have refused; for I was overcome at such a great lady's offering her arm to a poor girl like me!' Then she added, 'It's true, the honour of the religious life is far above the grandeurs of the world.'

This last reflexion is characteristic of Jeanne's way of thinking, and she inspired her religious family with a deter-mination to disregard all artificial grandeur: birth, wealth, cultural polish. It is remarkable, for instance, to see a Jeanne-Marie Buis, formerly Mlle Morel's maid,[3] become a Superior almost immediately after joining the Congre-gation. It is certainly a Gospel precept, but one often ignored; Jeanne Jugan and her companions for their part had thoroughly grasped it.

In any case, Jeanne was in no danger of forgetting that she was only a *poor girl*: pains were taken to remind her of it. One profession-day, Fr Le Pailleur was addressing all the Little Sisters in the hall; he 'paid compliments to the

[3] See Chapter 16, above.

aged Sisters who were there, mentioning them by name and saying that they were the pillars of the Congregation. He forbore to mention Sister Mary of the Cross who was present and who did not show the least emotion.' In similar circumstances, however, she was overheard to murmur, as though talking to herself, 'I began the work, all the same!' But no one ever heard her utter one bitter or rebellious word.

At most, a cry of contained grief. One day, with her head in her hands, she is reported to have said, 'They have stolen my work from me!' On other occasions, as we have seen, she repeated these words as a joke when talking to the Abbé Le Pailleur, '*Good Father*, you have stolen my work from me! But I willingly give it to you . . . '

Certainly she was represented and treated almost as though she were a *simpleton*. One novice saw her mercilessly snubbed. She replied calmly, 'Thank you, *good Mother*.' She was left absolutely on her own, ignored by Fr Le Pailleur and the Council; she never attended meetings, receptions or family celebrations; the Superiors never asked her to come and see them. The name days of the Mothers and the *good Father* were observed with solemnity and joy; hers, never. 'At La Tour, she was just a *little old woman*, whom nobody bothered about.' But she could see the work as blessed by God, and Christ being glorified in it; this was her joy. 'He must increase and I must decrease.'

She was aware that, when the *small beginnings* of the Congregation were taught in the novitiate, the young Sisters were told not to believe what was said in the outside world: that she was the foundress, the first Little Sister. She had been received two years after the work started, she was not the one who had gone to fetch the first old woman; true, the old woman had been taken into her house, which had thus served as the original refuge, but Fr Le Pailleur

paid for it all at the rate of 600 francs a year.[4] The majority
of the young Sisters found this easy to believe.

But others were astounded, and a more or less clandestine tradition seems always to have existed among the
young recruits: some of them *knew*, through their families!
A postulant from Saint-Servan said to her one day, 'My
good Little Sister, you were the first Little Sister!' Normally
she was able to parry this sort of question with a smile:
'This little girl wants to know everything!' But this time,
caught off her guard, she replied, 'I was the third Little
Sister!' 'No, you were the first one, Mamma told me!'
Usually when she was asked about her true role, she would
refuse to answer. 'They'll tell you about that in the novitiate.' Sometimes she would add, as though seeing beyond
the horizon, 'Later, you'll know all about that.' To some
Little Sisters who were going to Saint-Servan, she said,
'People will talk to you about me, but let the matter drop.
God knows all.' Well she knew his measure, in whom she
put her trust.

An attempt seems to have been made to get her to sign
a statement declaring that she was not the foundress or the
first Little Sister, but she apparently refused. She could not
become an accomplice to this lie!

At a certain period, a few Little Sisters observed a kind
of uneasiness in her, possibly corresponding to the uneasiness of the young, who could not bear *to see her pensioned
off, as it were, and cast aside*, while unable to refute this
official lie. But this is an isolated testimony; many, many
others, contrariwise, throughout those years at La Tour
insist on her extreme charm of manner, her smile, her
spontaneity of approach. She would go and see the Little
Sisters at their work and have amusing or affectionate
things to say; in the wash-house for instance, 'I'm very

[4] We now see that these assertions, especially the last ones, were absolutely
untrue.

glad to see you've got big strong arms and know just what to do with the washing-beater.'

Her own experience, and what she saw others going through, inspired her with reflexions on humility of heart, on authority and obedience. 'When you are *in charge* [i.e. a Superior],' she used to say, 'if you don't know how to keep your little station, you rob God.'

One day, she said to a group of novices, 'If God were to put a little child in the office of First Superior, I should obey him.' Her love for the Church appeared in this question, which she used to ask from time to time, 'Suppose someone asked you which you love more, our Father Superior or the Holy Father, you should answer: our Holy Father above all! . . . All good things come to us from the Church.*

'Make the most of your novitiate: be fervent, be faithful to our holy Rule.' And she would add these words, wrung from long and secret suffering, 'You will never know what it has cost . . . ' Such glimpses of her inner life are invaluable. The overall impression left of her during this period is one of serenity and even gaiety. 'She was always cheerful.' Neither humiliation nor physical infirmity could spoil this peace.

To all appearance, says a novice of the time, 'she lived in the presence of God, and was always talking to us about him. Meeting us, she would say, "Work for God alone." We sensed that she was speaking from the fulness of her heart.' She used to talk about God enthusiastically, tenderly. 'She would be on fire when talking to us about God.'

Did she hear about an article published in *Le Temps* at the end of 1874? It is not impossible that the Fathers, who loved her well, may have read her extracts from it. It was, after a somewhat fanciful account of the origins, a description of the Paris house in the rue Notre-Dame des Champs. Speaking of the Little Sisters, it said, they 'have stayed

faithful to the great-hearted tradition of Jeanne
Jugan—they think of nothing but their poor; they efface
themselves behind them; they set no store by themselves.'

In 1875, Mgr d'Outremont came to preside over the
clothing of a Little Sister, Georgette du Coëtlosquet. For
Jeanne, this was a reminder of the beginnings of the house
in Tours, and in any case he spoke of this in his sermon.
The Vicomte du Coëtlosquet and his family asked to see
her. She said to the novice who was with her, 'Come along,
I shall have to go, but whatever shall I say to these grand
people? I shall talk to them about Providence!' To talk
about God's prevenient goodness, she was never at a loss.

It seems she used to stand in God's presence, at once
completely humble and completely familiar. Perhaps this
was what she meant to convey in one of those fine sayings
which she used to invent, 'You must be very little before
God. When you pray, begin like this. Imagine yourself like
a little frog before God.'

SOURCES FOR CHAPTER 29

MANUSCRIPT SOURCES

Archives des Petites Sœurs des Pauvres. Testimony of Little Sisters
of the Poor : Sœur Cécile de la Nativité reported by Sœur Aman-
dine de Marie, Sœur Isabelle de Saint Paul reported by Sœur
Alexis de Sainte Thérèse, Sœur Marcienne reported by Sœur
Marie Archange, Sœur Adrienne de Marie, Sœur Aimée de Saint
François, Sœur Alexis de Sainte Thérèse, Sœur Amandine de
Marie, Sœur Anatolie du Saint-Sacrement, Sœur Angélique de
Sainte Marie, Sœur Angélique de Saint Paul, Sœur Arsène
Alexis, Sœur Auguste Alexis, Sœur Blanche de Sainte Marie,
Sœur Donatienne de Saint François, Sœur Esther de Saint Paci-

fique, Sœur Honorine de la Trinité, Sœur Ignace de Saint Joseph, Sœur Ignace de Sainte Marie, Sœur Léocadie Marie, Sœur Léonce de la Nativité, Sœur Louisa de Saint Ambroise, Sœur Ludivine de Saint François, Sœur Marie de Sainte Marguerite, Sœur Marie Berchmans, Sœur Marie de Sainte Blandine, Sœur Marie Hortense, Sœur Michel Octave, Sœur Odile Marie, Sœur Onésime de la Nativité, Sœur Saint Albert, Sœur Saint Michel.

PRINTED SOURCES CONTEMPORARY WITH JEANNE JUGAN

Le Temps, 30 December 1874.

LATER STUDIES

H. Ram (Mme Abel), *The Little Sisters of the Poor,* London, Longmans, 1894; and *Les Petites Sœurs des Pauvres ou la Merveille du XIXe siècle,* Paris, Plon, 1895 (the latter being almost a translation of the former).

Dictionnaire de Théologie Catholique (Letouzey and Ané), art. *Nouet* (Jacques, S.J.)

30

'NOW ALL I CAN SEE IS GOD'

(1877–9)

A young Little Sister who arrived in the novitiate in November 1877 was almost immediately given the duty of helping Sister Mary of the Cross. Her first meeting left a deep impression on her. 'The Little Sister was in her arm-chair, praying or thinking . . . I was somewhat intimidated by her extreme thinness, her austere look, and her eyes which were of necessity almost shut; she could only see a little higher by throwing her head well back; the nerves of her eyelids seemed to be paralysed.'

Whenever a Little Sister came to visit her in her big room during the winter, the first thing she did as often as not was to glance at the fire. Jeanne would then say, 'You are too kind, all of you. I can look after my fire myself; a small one's enough for me.'

For the last two or three years of her life, Jeanne was almost blind. She often had to be guided to where she wanted to be. She could neither read nor work; her rosary never left her. Several Sisters of the period mention her evident tenderness for Mary, '*It was a pleasure* to see her praying with her rosary. She loved to say, "By the Ave Maria we shall get to Paradise!" '

'When you are old, you won't be able to see anymore. Now all I can see is God,' she used to tell the young Sisters. Or again: 'God can see me; that's enough!'

But when she spoke, her face would light up. There was

something radiant about her smile. She seemed fuller of
happiness than ever. Her voice was evidently not too
cracked, and she could not restrain herself from singing.
One novice remembered her very clearly, 'She was walking
down the path . . . and was singing so simply and happily,
waving her little stick in the air . . . She looked so simple
and happy!'

During the summer of 1877, she would join the novices
for recreation. She used to give out the straw hats, keeping
the worst one for herself, to make them laugh when she put
it on. She used to go out for walks with them. At this
period, she could still manage a kilometre or two. The
Little Sisters in charge used to make sure that each in turn
had a chance to enjoy her conversation. She still held
herself very straight, in her patched clothes, her big shoes
and her cape which by now had turned rather green. Being
tall, she impressed the novices by her remarkably firm
bearing; it was, one of them remarked of her, 'as though
she were always in the presence of God'.

Yet there was no affectation. She used to sing to amuse
them. One day it was an old song from her childhood, the
Cuckoo Song: 'Cuc-koo, put him in the stew!'[1] Another time,
the *Song of the Trades*; she emphasised its catchy rhythm by
vigorously beating time with her little stick.

She used to tell amusing anecdotes from her past, for
instance the story about a rabbit which she had been given
when out collecting. Delighted at the thought of taking it
home to her poor children, she forgot to fasten the basket-
lid. The prisoner jumped out of the basket. There were
some little boys standing by, who raced after the rabbit
and caught it, and she gave them a halfpenny apiece.

She would gaily warble a sort of counting-song, which
she had possibly made up herself:

[1] Lit.: *Cou-cou . . . coupez-lui le cou.* This memory dates from slightly earlier
(1874–5).

    For little maids who beg their food,
        Everything is always good.
    If you want to get on fast,
        Scorn for yourself you must show.
    Be very humble to the last
        And trample hard on your E-go!

Or:

    Never refuse anything,
        Do not pick and choose.
    For us little beggar-maids
        All things have their use!

Or again:

    Jesu blest,
    King of the Elect,
    Who will be the one to love you best?[2]

One Easter Day, some Little Sisters had assembled in the tribune to sing. Sister Mary of the Cross joined them. 'Come on, little ones, let's sing the glory of our risen Jesus!' Then, giving the beat with sweeping movements of both arms, she sang *Alleluia* with such ardour that she looked as though she wanted *to leave her old body and follow her Jesus*!

What spirit this old woman had!

Her youth was as though renewed in the atmosphere of thanksgiving pervading her. Like a refrain, she would say, 'In all things, everywhere, in all circumstances, I repeat: Blessed be God!' In the spring of 1879 it rained for weeks on end; there was anxiety over the hay. She met a Little Sister: 'What is the weather like today, little one?' 'It's raining, my good Little Sister Mary of the Cross.' 'Ah,

---

[2] The counting-songs have been grouped together here; they occur, with a few variants, in the testimonies of Sisters who knew her between 1868 and 1879. See also Chapter 27.

well, my child, we must always say: Blessed be God,
Blessed be God!'

Hundreds of times, but with ever-renewed joy, she was
heard to say, 'Love God truly, little one, love God truly.
God is so good!' She walked with God. Once more, she
took up this theme with one of the novices: 'I always begin
by putting myself in the presence of my God, so as to do
everything in his holy presence.'

Spontaneously, she associated her body, even in old age
(and perhaps even more so then!) with her transports of
prayer. A Little Sister had come to see her in the infirmary
and they were chatting together. They heard the bell ring
out at Benediction of the Blessed Sacrament. Then she
prostrated herself, saying, 'My God, how great, how good
you are! You deign to bless so great a sinner as me. I adore
you, I love you, have pity on me!'

She went on receiving visits right to the end: from old
friends, or even from unknown people who wanted to have
seen *Jeanne Jugan*. When people told her this, she would
answer, 'Don't go on calling me Jeanne Jugan. Jeanne
Jugan has been dead for nearly forty years. All that's left
now is Sister Mary of the Cross, unworthy though she is
of that lovely name.' The death of Jeanne Jugan had indeed
occurred with the imposition of her name in religion (4
February 1844)—but, more so, in the years that followed,
with the progressive deprivation of everything that had
made her famous, a deprivation to which she had magnan-
imously assented. No longer, in any way, did she have
proprietary rights over the person known as *Jeanne Jugan*,
nor had the latter over her. She was free, rejoicing before
God and before men to be the utterly little, utterly poor
and utterly new Sister Mary of the Cross.

On 19 March 1877, there were a great many guests at
La Tour Saint-Joseph for the patronal festival. Among
them, Madame de La Corbinière who, long ago, thirty-five

years before, when she was only twelve, had been to visit
the *Big Downstairs*. She observed that Sister Mary of the
Cross was not taking part in the festivities. But the visitors
kept asking for her and in the end she was brought along;
she was greeted with rapture.

> She carries her eighty-four years valiantly. I found her reju-
> venated, to my way of thinking, for I had expected to see her
> pretty far gone. Not at all: she is upright and still retains all
> her faculties . . . I was very pleased that, in memory of my
> father, she should have chosen me to replace her postulant.
> Leaning on my arm, this good old woman took a few turns
> with me in the alleys and courtyards . . .
>
> I felt very proud to have this venerable Mother to myself.
> Although I did ask her one or two questions, I could see that
> she was used to conversing with God—and what conversation
> could be preferable to that?

Another day, it was one of her great-nieces[3] who came
to see her. She later related,

> I was then fifteen or sixteen . . . I can still see my very tall
> aunt. What struck me about her was her humility. She asked,
> if the street was named after her, that this should not be done.
> She asked me, 'Are you coming to live here with me one day,
> little Aline?' . . . I asked her how many times she said her
> rosary each day: she was always praying. And the Little Sisters
> whom we met—how sweetly she smiled at them!

Sometimes, when the novitiate went out for a walk—an
immense party of six hundred young people, distributed
over three years—she would put herself at the window of
her big room, smiling and waving to them. It made her so
happy to see them setting out on the road which God had
originally shown her. The Little Sisters responded with
much affectionate waving and even a little jostling; and

---

[3] Aline Derrien, daughter of Perrine Emery, grand-daughter of Thérèse-Charlotte
Joucan.

this was not always to the taste of the Little Sisters-in-charge.

Her favourites were the novices who had come from America. The others were a little jealous of the attention which she lavished on them. But she regarded them as the little family's first *missionaries*; they had spent sixteen days on the ocean, and it was heroic of young girls to leave their families so far away and to sacrifice their native tongue; they had to have a double vocation to do it! She used to worry about whether these young Americans were warm enough, whether they had enough to eat. Since they were unused to working in the fields and were nervous of rough-spoken Brother Julian the overseer, Jeanne used to encourage and reassure them.

We have already heard her speaking on many occasions about the aged poor. In these years, thinking back over her own life, she would often revert to this topic in her conversations with the novices. She tried to pass on to them something of what God had given her. 'When you are with the Poor, give yourselves with all your heart.' We have written *Poor* with a capital, since there was complete identity, for her, between the aged person standing there and Jesus, of whom the pauper is a member. One of her favourite songs was:

> The Poor Man is calling us
> Aloud and from his heart—
> Oh, what Glad Tidings!
> Now gladly we'll set out.

'When she came into the sewing-room, she would tell us that she was glad to see us mending the linen and clothing. "For, you know, we are often given old linen and worn-out clothes. We must learn how to make poverty look respectable!" ' Thus, even doing the mending was an occasion for her to live the respect due to all those loved by God.

A young kitchen-Sister used sometimes to bring her her meals. Jeanne often used to give her scraps of advice on how to deal with the poor.

You mustn't begrudge your efforts in cooking for them any-more than in looking after them when they are ill. Be like a mother to the grateful ones, and also to those who don't know how to be grateful for everything you do for them. Say in your heart, 'I do it for you, my Jesus!' Look on the Poor with compassion, and Jesus will look kindly on you in your last day.

She would add suggestions for moments of crisis,

Go and find him when your patience and strength give out and you feel alone and helpless. Jesus is waiting for you in the chapel. Say to him, 'Jesus, you know exactly what is going on. You are all I have, and you know all. Come to my help.' And then go, and don't worry about how you are going to manage. That you have told God about it is enough. He has a good memory.

As well as being advice, this was undoubtedly a guarded reference to her own behaviour.

Again, she would say, 'The bread of the poor is the bread of God.' And again, like a refrain, 'Be kind, little ones, to the infirm.' 'Do not be afraid of devoting yourselves to, and of begging for, the poor as I have done, for they are the suffering members of Our Lord.'

And she would sing the praises of voluntary poverty, 'Poverty is my treasure . . . It is so beautiful being poor, having nothing, awaiting all from God . . . O holy Poverty! Love her well and she will always keep you, for God loves her and will bless those who keep her.' Or again: 'If we only knew what riches are ours, how we should love our poor mended clothes and our poor food!'

And she would tirelessly recommend that other form of poverty—humility of heart, 'Be very little, very humble!'

'Be little, little, little; if you get big, the Congregation will fall!' 'Dear little ones, work hard at your novitiate, be truly fervent. Above all, learn to be truly humble and, once you go to a house, be truly little, for if you truly keep the spirit of the little family, the spirit of humility, of simplicity, of littleness, not seeking the esteem of the great, then you will give cause for other people to bless God and you will obtain the conversion of souls. On the other hand, were you to become big and proud, the Congregation would fall!' 'Only the little are pleasing to God.' *Littleness* was her key-word.

Thinking of these young Sisters' future responsibilities, she would advise them to practise prayerful reflexion. 'Little ones, you must pray and think before you act. I myself have done this all my life. I used to weigh my every word.' And she would recall how, when beginning any work, she would try to foresee how it would develop and what the consequences would be. She taught them this prayer: 'Mother of Wisdom, pray for us!' And she would add, 'You will need all the wisdom you can get when you are collecting-Sisters!'

We have lingered at some length over Jeanne's advice and reflexions, since these seem particularly important in this final period of her life: as though she felt the urgency of passing on her message in its entirety, before she left her young sisters. As though this were, in a certain sense, her testament.

Apparently, in the last year of her life, she became rather bent; at certain times, at least, she appeared to observers as though bent over her stick. But she was still able to go for long walks in the park. Witness this incident in the spring of 1879: Three little boys, ranging from ten to four years old (all three of them later became priests) espied some luscious strawberry-beds through the hedge. There was no one about. They made a hole through the hedge and set to work eating the juicy fruit. Suddenly the eldest one made off, for there was Sister Mary of the Cross bearing down on them, brandishing her stick! The youngest, who was probably more absorbed, saw her quite close up: 'You little rascal!' She must have had a nice smile, for he could not remember having felt afraid. All the same, he had retained and possibly exaggerated the memory of her silhouette: *tall, very tall, thin, bony, and an austere face.*

During this last year, she had a visit from M. de Kervers, whose father had helped her at Saint-Servan. His daughter, Marie de Kervers, relates how Jeanne,

> with sly delight, enjoyed teasing him by reminding him of the tricks and practical jokes which the roguish little boy, as he then was, used to play on her. The venerable woman was leaning on a stick, the handle of which had been bound with some bits of rag to make it softer to her aged hand. Seeing this, my father said to her, 'Dear Jeanne, I don't want you to use that nasty stick. All the while I'm here, do me the honour of leaning on my arm.' 'Oh, Mister Edmond, you always were a one to have your own way!' And in high spirits she walked about the estate on my father's arm.

A few months before, in July 1878, the Chapter of the Congregation had met at La Tour. One hundred and thirty-seven *capitulars* represented the one hundred and seventy houses then in existence throughout the world. Inside the chapter-room, they were about to proceed to the election of the Mother Superior-General. The *novices of the plainchant* were standing outside in a group, waiting to go in and sing the *Te Deum*. Sister Mary of the Cross had been brought along with them. They were passing the time of day. In response to some question or other put to her, Jeanne laughingly said, 'But of course, I'm going to wait here with you . . . though really I ought to be inside!'

She must have been very much at peace with herself by this time, to be able to joke like this on this topic. And we are lucky to have a glimpse of her laughing at herself in this last period of her life when, it would appear, she was, as it were, invaded by joy.

SOURCES FOR CHAPTER 30

MANUSCRIPT SOURCES

Archives des Petites Sœurs des Pauvres. Testimony of Little Sisters of the Poor : Sœur Adrienne de Marie, Sœur Aimée de Saint François, Sœur Anatolie du Saint-Sacrement, Sœur Angèle Marie, Sœur Angélique de Sainte Marie, Sœur Anne de Sainte Marie, Sœur Apollinaire du Saint-Sacrement, Sœur Arsène de Saint Jean, Sœur Augustine de Saint Laurent, Sœur Catherine de tous les Saints, Sœur Cécile de Saint Pierre, Sœur Céline de l'Ascension, Sœur Christine de la Providence, Sœur Denise de Saint Joseph, Sœur Donatienne de Saint François, Sœur Emmanuel de Saint Etienne, Sœur Eulalie de la Présentation, Sœur Hedwige, Sœur Hortense de Sainte Anne, Sœur Ignace de Sainte Marie, Sœur Léocadie Marie, Sœur Léonce de la Nativité, Sœur Léontine de la Nativité, Sœur Louise de l'Immaculée, Sœur Marguerite de Sainte Marie, Sœur Marie-Hortense, Sœur Marie-Rosalie, Sœur Marie de Saint Bernardin, Sœur Marie de Sainte Blandine, Sœur Marie de Sainte Marguerite, Sœur Marie de Saint Romain, Sœur Melaine de Saint Louis, Sœur Nathalie de la Résurrection, Sœur Pascaline, Sœur Raymond, Sœur Sainte Alodie, Sœur Saint Aurélien, Sœur Saint Michel, Sœur Séraphine du Saint-Esprit, Sœur Sidonie de Sainte Anne, Sœur Ursule du Sacré-Cœur, Sœur Valentine Joseph. Letters of Fr Lelièvre.

Other testimony : Mlle de Kervers, Mme Serneguet, Ch. Mathurin Durand.

STUDIES

C. de La Corbinière, op. cit.
A. Helleu, op. cit.

31

FROM DEATH TO LIFE

(1879)

Jeanne was longing for the day when she would at last be with God in Light. A Little Sister had come to keep her company. She was going out again after a few minutes' conversation, when Jeanne said to her, 'Sing me the refrain, *Oh why on this alien shore, must I prolong my stay? . . .* '

She would say to the young, 'I long to die, to go and see God!' 'You mustn't die!' 'Yes, yes, I want to; I want to go and see God.' She used to make them pray every day that God would grant her the grace of a good death.

She may perhaps have heard about Bernadette Soubirous' death, which occurred on 16 April 1879.[1] A novice died at about the same time; Jeanne comforted the others: 'Come along now, little ones, be brave! One of us has left for Glory; our own turn will come. We must be prepared. We must love God truly. Today is a day of joy over our Little Sister's entry into Heaven.' As she spoke, her serene faith could be seen; her face seemed to radiate light.

For many years, her principal task had been to watch over her religious family in continual, supplicatory, marvelling prayer. More than ever she thought, 'God will help us; the work is his.' And she was well aware that she would pursue this same mission in the light beyond the threshold

[1] That year, the death also occurred, in Lyons, though slightly after Jeanne's, of Fr Antoine Chevrier, another poor servant of the poor (2 October 1879).

of death. But perhaps she still had one desire left: before she died to see her Congregation's constitutions approved by the Pope.

In November 1878, Fr Lelièvre had been sent to Rome, charged with the responsibility of soliciting the Holy See's approbation of the constitutions of the Little Sisters of the Poor (the first approbation, obtained on 9 July 1854, had only been *ad experimentum*).

He was received in audience by Leo XIII. With him, he had the file containing the letters of the bishops. The Pope read one or two of them there and then, and listened to what he had to say on the Congregation's behalf. He asked, 'And now, your Superiors would like to ask for approbation of the Rule? Is that what they want?'

> Above all, they wish to conform to your Holiness's views in this matter. There is one point in the constitutions of the Little Sisters of the Poor by which the Superiors set great store and which I, like them, believe to be of the highest importance. It is the one concerning the conservation of poverty as it is now practised. According to the constitutions, the houses may have no capital, no regular sources of income and no regular allocations from the civil administration. They have to be entirely dependent on the alms of the faithful and the Sisters' collections.

The Pope gave his approval on this point and told Fr Lelièvre to hand the documents over to the Congregation concerned. The latter gave careful study to the articles dealing with poverty and the vow of hospitality.

Finally, on 1 March 1879, the Pope approved the constitutions of the Little Sisters of the Poor for seven years. At that moment, there were two thousand four hundred Little Sisters.

Jeanne had completed her work; she could depart.

In the course of the summer of 1879, she seemed to grow

weaker. On 27 or 28 August,[2] she saw her confessor and received God's forgiveness from him. He was struck, that day, by how lively, how very much all there she was.

Next morning, after Mass, she had an attack. She was put to bed. She recovered consciousness and was given the Sacrament of the Sick. She was able to pray in a low voice: 'O Mary, you know you are my mother, do not forsake me! ... Eternal Father, open your gates today to the most wretched of your little daughters, to one though who most earnestly longs to see you!' and in a fainter voice, 'O Mary, my dear mother, come to me. You know I love you and how I long to see you!' Then she quietly passed away.

There was something so calm and reposeful about her on her death-bed, that they found it hard to tear their eyes away.

SOURCES FOR CHAPTER 31

MANUSCRIPT SOURCES

Archives des Petites Sœurs des Pauvres. Testimony of Little Sisters of the Poor : Sœur Adèle de Sainte Marie, Sœur Aimée de Saint François, Sœur Blanche de Sainte Marie, Sœur Céline de l'Ascension, Sœur Delphine de Saint Jean, Sœur Léonce de la Nativité, Sœur Louise de l'Immaculée, Sœur Saint-Michel, Sœur Thérèse Augustine.

[2] There is doubt over the date of her death. The entries in the death and burial registers bear the same date, 29 August. This must be a mistake, since it is most unlikely that she would have been buried on the very day she died. There is testimony to suggest that she died on 28 August, the feast of St Augustine and hence a particularly solemn feast for the Abbé Auguste Le Pailleur. Rather than upset the feast, Sister Mary of the Cross's death may have been kept a secret until the following day. No announcement of her death appeared in any circular letter. A year later, the Abbé le Pailleur made a passing allusion to her as 'his third spiritual daughter', adding, 'who died here a short while ago'.

Livre de fondation of the mother-house. Letters of Fr Lelièvre. Circular letters of Fr Le Pailleur, in particular that of 31 August 1880.

STUDIES

C. de La Corbinière, op. cit.
A. Leroy, op. cit.

32

'FROM FAITH TO FAITH'

Jeanne Jugan had acquitted herself of her mission. She had
completed it all, simply, without phrase-making. Now she
fell asleep to be born into Light.

In this final, hidden phase of her life, we have first seen
her brought to a halt in mid-career, and out of obedience
go into hiding behind the walls of the mother-house. A new
form of deprivation, in which she experienced what it
means *to be grafted on to the Cross*. At La Piletière and then
at La Tour Saint-Joseph, she performed humble tasks often
difficult to identify; but she lived among the young, passing
on to them in chance encounters that wisdom knitted up
in her over many years; to them she communicated her
own absolute faith in God as Love, and her own preoccupation with the Poor. On one sole occasion she took part
in a meeting of the council of her Congregation, and then
to influence a vital decision concerning poverty—trusting
in God alone, the Little Sisters of the Poor would have no
regular income. We sense her constant attentiveness, her
loving attentiveness to her young sisters, her awareness of
God's working in the world, and of God's presence in her.
More and more peacefully, she endures the unjust way in
which she is kept ignored and without any sort of responsibility. She makes herself little, very little—yet is magnan-
imous, fully responsible before God for her work, and
overflowing with thanksgiving for the gifts which he lavishes on her. More and more free, and simply happy, she

looks forward to dying so that she can see God. Her task done, she takes her leave, 'Now, Master, you can let your servant go in peace.'

Let us try and take an overall view of the spiritual road which she follows. We might throw light on it, I think, by using a free interpretation of a somewhat mysterious expression of St Paul: she goes 'from faith to faith' (Rm 1:17). We might also say of her that she goes from poverty to poverty; or again, from poverty to faith, from faith to poverty, and so on. For in her life's song, poverty constitutes a kind of counterpoint inseparable from faith.[1]

As a child, she knew want and insecurity; very young, she had to earn her own living at menial tasks: not for her to become bogged down in possessions and comfort. She was free to undertake the long adventure of faith, the quest for God.

Prayerfully, she lives out the silence and lengthy waiting. Her faith matures. It leads her, summons by summons, to a new kind of poverty: Jeanne leaves her family, renounces the chance of getting married, pledges herself to serve the poor. So doing, and living a life of communion and sharing, according to the motion of Love shed in her heart by the Holy Spirit (Rm 5:5), and contemplating him, too, in Jesus Christ, she comes to know God better. She comes to a clearer understanding of God's plan on earth, where there are so many poor people. Following Christ's, her gaze rests for preference on those wounded, lonely creatures waiting for her smile and a bit of comfort.

Then, after a short respite, urged by 'the charity of Christ' (2 Co 5:14), she takes another step forward, hazarding her own destiny, no longer merely to be at the service of the poor, but to be with them. The decisive acts of giving

---

[1] A theme well developed by Cardinal Garrone in his fine book, *Ce que croyait Jeanne Jugan*, Tours, Mame, 1974; trans. *Poor in Spirit, the spirituality of Jeanne Jugan*, London, Darton, Longman & Todd, 1975.

up her bed and of going out begging on their behalf, made her really and truly poor with the poor.

But the more she involved herself like this—henceforth beyond the bounds of common sense—the nearer to God she felt herself to be, living by him, carried by him. Sure of him. She was sure, in faith, that this sharing, this absolute solidarity with the aged poor was God's life within her. Hence she had no choice but to go forward, boldly relying on him alone, without other security. Since God as Love wished it within her, that was what she had to do. The more she loved in God, the more she became convinced by faith that God would never forsake his poor, whom he loved in her.

God proposed to her that she should go further along this path of believing poverty and stark faith. He led her to consent, without losing hope, to being 'robbed of her work' and even of the truth about her role in the origin of that work. God would take care of that. New depths of faith.

And in the final phase of her existence, ignored and set aside, humbly mingling with the young Little Sisters and full of love for them, she allows the Spirit of Jesus to bring her faith to fruit in wisdom, in love of the Poor, and in joy.

Deep, smiling wisdom: the expression of a truly spiritual, liberating, inner renunciation; loving contemplation of Christ and continual reference to him 'until he were formed in her' (Gal 4:19); prudence, moderation, discretion; prayer at once supplicatory and marvelling, continual and wide open to the world; enthusiastic love of God, of his Presence; familiarity with the Bridegroom. An ardent desire to see him, at the last.

Love of the poor too, who are at the same time Jesus in his poverty; an immense respect for all beings loved by God; confidence in the Passover mystery at work in them; careful, resourceful, tactful care for the welfare and happiness of each one of them; the desire to be with them in littleness, which is where God is free to love us.

Lastly, joy, seeming totally to invade her as poverty makes her progressively freer and creates in her a kind of connivance with God; thanksgiving, already permeating her youth, becomes more vibrant; in her latter years she exults even in body, worn out yet set free; often cheerful and singing, she knows and radiates a peaceful serenity; her face, when she smiles, is luminous.

Making her share by love the distress of the poor, the Spirit has brought her, by these very means, into the depths of God and of his joy.

And thus she learnt, and thus she teaches us, the blessedness of the poor,

> *Blessed are the poor*
> *for the Kingdom of God*
>   —which is God himself,
>   with all his joy, his freedom, his tenderness—
> *the Kingdom of God*
> *is theirs.*

APPENDICES

I BIBLIOGRAPHY OF PRINCIPAL SOURCES FOR THE LIFE OF JEANNE JUGAN

A complete list of sources known today and a comprehensive bibliography are to be found in the volume entitled *Positio super virtutibus servae Dei Ioannae Jugan*, published in the context of the Process for Beatification. We only give the major documents here.

MANUSCRIPT SOURCES

1 *Mémoire adressé à l'Académie française en vue de l'attribution du Prix Montyon*
Archives of the Académie française. Photograph and microfilm in the Archives of the Little Sisters of the Poor. Drawn up in 1844 by the notables of Saint-Servan and written in the Abbé Le Pailleur's hand, this is a key document for information on the history of the origins of the Congregation of the Little Sisters of the Poor.

2 *Correspondance et notes des premières Petites Sœurs des Pauvres.*
Archives of the Little Sisters of the Poor. Unfortunately the collection is not complete.

3 *Livres de fondation* of the first houses; *livre du conseil général*.
Archives of the Little Sisters of the Poor. The originals are no longer in existence : only somewhat touched-up copies; even so these are valuable sources.

4 *Circulaires* of the Abbé Le Pailleur.

5 *Registres des délibérations et des correspondances* of the Mayor of Saint-Servan.

Saint-Servan Municipal Archives. In particular, debate of 28 May 1866 on the *rue Jeanne Jugan*.

6 *Testimonies of Little Sisters of the Poor* who knew Jeanne Jugan.

Archives of the Little Sisters of the Poor. These testimonies are either direct, or transmitted by other people. They arrived in several waves:

a) Answers to an invitation from Sœur Marguerite de Saint Augustin Geny, Superior-General: 1912–16.

b) Answers to an invitation from Sœur Marguerite-Marie du Sacré-Cœur Laure, Superior-General: 1932–6.

c) 176 answers to the enquiry of the Vice-Postulator charged with conducting the preliminary Diocesan Investigation with a view to Beatification: 1935.

d) Depositions of Little Sisters at the Diocesan Investigation.

7 *Testimonies of other persons* who knew Jeanne Jugan.

Archives of the Little Sisters of the Poor. These testimonies have for the most part been transmitted by the families of these persons, in the context of the Diocesan Investigation (1935).

8 *Études manuscrites* of the Abbé Leroy, in particular : *Détails se rapportant à 'Histoire et Œuvre' des Petites Sœurs des Pauvres.*

Archives of the Little Sisters of the Poor.

9 *Études manuscrites* of Canon Helleu, in particular: *Notes et observations relatives à certains documents faisant partie du dossier de la cause de Jeanne Jugan.*

Archives of the Little Sisters of the Poor.

PRINTED SOURCES CONTEMPORARY WITH JEANNE JUGAN'S LIFE

1 The article by the English tourist who visited Dinan in 1846. Unfortunately, the text of this is not extant, but only a translation; it is printed in A. L. Masson, *Les premières Petites Sœurs des*

Pauvres, Lyon, Vitte, 1899; the author says that he found the article in 'an old review'. The same translation, with a few cuts and minor stylistic adjustments, is found in A. Leroy, *Histoire des Petites Sœurs des Pauvres*, Paris, Poussielgue, 1902.

2 Y. Tennaëc (= A. Chevremont) *La destinée du pauvre.*
Stances dédiées à Jeanne Jugan, Rennes, Marteville, 1846.
Reprinted in *Clairières*, Rennes, Marteville, 1848; Paris, Paul Servan, 1873.

3 Numerous local newspaper articles, especially between 1846 and 1851, at Rennes, Dinan, Saint-Brieuc, Tours, Angers. Specific references are given at the ends of relevant chapters of this book.

4 Louis Veuillot, *Les Petites Sœurs des Pauvres, ou le droit à l'assistance selon le christianisme*, in *l'Univers*, 13 September 1848. Reprinted in *Mélanges religieux, historiques, politiques et littéraires*, vol. IV, Paris, Vivès, 1857 and 1861. Re-issued and reworked in *Les libres penseurs*, 2nd edition, Paris, 1850. See note below.

5 Léon Aubineau, *Histoire des Petites Sœurs des Pauvres*, in *l'Univers*, 22 and 24 December 1851; 1 and 5 January 1852. Reproduced in the *Journal de Rennes*, 24, 25, 27, 28, 29, 31 January and 3 February 1852. Then published in book-form, Paris, Bailly, Divry et Cie, 1852; Nancy, Grimblot et Raybois, 1852; Nancy, Vagner, 1855; Lille, Lefort, 1852, 1859, 1863, 1867, 1868, 1873, 1877, 1879, 1882, 1884. Reproduced in *Les serviteurs de Dieu*, vol. I, Paris, Vaton, 1852; Paris, Lethielleux, 1860; Paris, Palmé, 1875, 1880, 1888. Various editions and translations outside France. See note below.

6 Ch. Dickens, *The Little Sisters*, in *Household Words, a weekly journal conducted by Charles Dickens*, 14 February 1852. He describes a visit to the house in the rue Saint-Jacques in Paris and shows himself accurately informed on the origins of the Congregation.

LATER STUDIES

1 C. de La Corbinière, *Jeanne Jugan et les Petites Sœurs des Pauvres*, with an introduction by L. Aubineau, Paris, Lecoffre, 1883; 2nd ed. 1895. See note below.

2 A. Leroy, *Histoire des Petites Sœurs des Pauvres*, Paris, Poussielgue, 1902. Translated into various languages. See note below.

3 A. Helleu, *Une grande bretonne, Jeanne Jugan, fondatrice des Petites Sœurs des Pauvres*, Rennes, Riou-Reuzé, 1938. See note below.

4 F. Trochu, *Jeanne Jugan, fondatrice des Petites Sœurs des Pauvres*, Lyon, Vitte, 1947; 2nd ed., La Tour Saint-Joseph, 1961. Translated into several languages. A work of talent, elaborating on the labours of Canon Helleu. A few inaccuracies of detail.

5 Cardinal G. M. Garrone, *Ce que croyait Jeanne Jugan*, Tours, Mame, 1974; *Poor in Spirit* London, Darton, Longman & Todd, 1975. Translated into several languages. A meditation on the dual yet unitary life of faith and poverty led by Jeanne Jugan.

II   BRIEF CRITICAL NOTES ON JEANNE JUGAN'S EARLIEST BIOGRAPHERS

LOUIS VEUILLOT (1813–83)

Catholic journalist, editor-in-chief of *L'Univers*. Frequently a violent polemicist.

He derived his information about Jeanne Jugan and the origins

of the Congregation from Marie Jamet, who received him at the
house in Tours in 1848. The first form of his account tallies with
the course of events as related in the *Memorial to the French
Academy*.

But in *Les Libres Penseurs*, 2nd edition, 1850, he reprinted his
article in a radically re-worked form, blurring the role played by
Jeanne and attributing the foundation to the Abbé Le Pailleur
and his two spiritual daughters, Marie Jamet and Virginie
Trédaniel. In the interval, he had probably met the Abbé Le
Pailleur, who had certainly been to Paris. Later he was to meet
Jeanne Jugan on a number of occasions, either at La Piletière or
at La Tour.

He reprinted the article in its original form in *Mélanges religieux,
historiques, politiques et littéraires*, vol. 4, 1857 and 1861. But he
accompanied it with a note: 'When I first had the honour and
pleasure of talking about the Little Sisters of the Poor and of
introducing them, so to speak, to a religious public which had
not as yet heard of them, I hardly knew them myself; at least, I
knew very little about their history. Dear Sister Jeanne Jugan
was not the foundress of this admirable family. She entered it
only as its third or fourth member. The Abbé Le Pailleur was
the founder . . . '

LEON AUBINEAU (1815–91)

Archivist, editor on *L'Univers*; president of the Society of St Vincent de Paul at Tours. It was he presumably who put Veuillot
in touch with the house in Tours.

He left Tours at the end of 1850 to settle in Paris. There he
met the Abbé Le Pailleur, to whom he submitted the manuscript
of the article which he intended to publish in *L'Univers*. Thus,
from the outset, his presentation of the origins attributes all the
initiative to the Abbé and his two spiritual daughters; Jeanne
was drawn in only gradually, joining them later.

Edition by edition, and more markedly in 1877, Aubineau
modified his text by reducing Jeanne's role more and more and
by exalting that played by the Abbé. Jeanne's attic becomes
Fanchon's attic and the latter moves into the foreground. Orig-

inally he spoke of 'four foundresses'; by the time he had finished, there was only one founder.

In the meanwhile, Léon Aubineau's sister-in-law had joined the Little Sisters of the Poor; she was professed at La Tour in 1865; Aubineau was presumably present and would have seen Jeanne then. The new religious was sent to Spain, dying there in 1872. Now, at that time, Aubineau was in financial difficulties, disaster having struck *L'Univers*. The Abbé Le Pailleur ceded him 40,000 francs, the total sum of his sister-in-law's legacy to the Congregation. After this, no doubt, Aubineau felt obliged to show his gratitude.

Jeanne Jugan died in 1879. In *L'Univers* of 31 August 1879, Aubineau devoted a long article to her, presenting the 'legend' in more than ever exaggerated form.

Even so, one point should be made. Though Aubineau gives an inaccurate account of the origins of the Little Sisters of the Poor, he professes a fervent admiration for Jeanne Jugan's virtues and greatness of soul and he has a gift for presenting these convincingly. His work has been quoted several times in the present study.

CLÉMENTINE DE LA CORBINIÈRE, née LE FER DE LA MOTTE (1829–95)

For many years Jeanne had been known and supported by Clémentine's father and other people close to her. In childhood and adolescence, she herself had known Jeanne at Saint-Servan. She saw her again in extreme old age at La Tour in 1877. From 1839 to 1846, the Abbé Le Pailleur had been her confessor and she admired him all her life.

The book is lively and imaginative, presented in the form of a fictitious correspondence. It is the only text to inform us about Jeanne's childhood and youth.

Mme de La Corbinère used excellent sources: she drew on her personal memories, those of her circle, the accounts of Jeanne's friend Anne Citré, and the recollections of Jeanne's sister Thérèse-Charlotte Emery as transmitted by the latter's daughters, Jeanne's nieces, who had themselves known Jeanne and admired her; also those of other witnesses whom she had questioned.

But she submitted her text to the Abbé Le Pailleur, who evidently emended it and also gave her a statement on the origins of the Congregation. Hence the several discrepancies in her story and, on occasion, her discreet expressions of surprise: she believed that things had happened otherwise.

A Little Sister who was working in the secretariat of the Congregation from 1880 to 1886 recorded what she remembered as regards Mme de La Corbinière's behaviour over her book: 'I know they sent for Mlle Le Fer de La Motte (Mme de La Corbinière), a very well-informed lady, and asked her not to have her little book published. She had it published all the same, but I am convinced that the contradictions appearing in the book are due to the pressure brought to bear on her' (Deposition of Sister Saint-Michel).

Sister Alexis de Sainte Thérèse, who knew Jeanne while she herself was a novice (1872–4), who saw her again at the General Chapter of 1878 and who later became Assistant General (1894), left some notes on this book. Here is the gist of them:

(a) It 'contains inaccuracies about the history of our Congregation. These are due, not to the author who wrote in good faith, but to tendencies of the day which sought to establish Marie Jamet as the first Little Sister . . . Efforts were made, despite many testimonies to the contrary, to deprive Jeanne of her primacy.'

(b) Nonetheless, 'on the evidence of the *facts*, the narrative itself makes it perfectly clear that Jeanne was certainly the one who had brought the Congregation into existence.' Indeed, the facts detailed give a thoroughgoing impression that Jeanne played a decisive role in the birth of the association, that she, as it were, personified it by her activities and virtues, that she inspired her companions with absolute trust in God's providence and the poverty concomitant with this, that she inaugurated the begging-round, stamping her own characteristic mark on it for ever, that she contributed decisively to the growth of the Congregation, after having herself taken in the first aged man. In a word, the facts related by Mme de La Corbinière contradict important points in the 'legend'.

(c) Lastly, Jeanne's personality seems to have been exactly captured in it: 'Jeanne Jugan's humble virtues . . . the no less humble facts of her career, cannot be disputed; . . . the author speaks of her with profound esteem; . . . and depicts the moral and physical features of Sister Mary of the Cross precisely as we ourselves remember them.'

ARSÈNE LEROY (1854–1919)

Priest, native of Bécherel (a large village near La Tour Saint-Joseph). In 1881, he became an associate of the auxiliary priests of the Little Sisters of the Poor. He came to know the Congregation, a fair number of its houses, and its history well. He may even have known Jeanne Jugan personally.

In 1894, at the request and with the encouragement of Sister Augustine de Saint André, Vicar-General of the Congregation of the Little Sisters of the Poor, he resolved to write an account of this history and amassed a great deal of information for the purpose. On the origins of the association he gathered direct testimony from a fair number of Sisters.

In particular, he received Marie Jamet's decisive statement. This he later passed on to Sister Marie de la Croix (Joséphine James), a religious of the Sisters of the Saints Cœurs de Jésus et de Marie of Paramé. 'Speaking to me', she relates, 'of Jeanne Jugan as foundress of the Congregation of the Little Sisters of the Poor, the Abbé Leroy, who was then our chaplain, told me, "I prepared Marie Jamet for death; this is what she said: *I was not the first one, but I was told to act as though I were*" ' (Note by Sister Marie de la Croix, 1942 and 1943).

The Abbé Leroy was a methodical worker, who subjected his sources to stringent critical analysis. He refused anything as fact which was not solidly attested by documentary evidence (see the note on the Eudist Third Order, Chapter 5, note 1 above).

Taking the *Memorial* addressed to the French Academy as his basis, he establishes the truth about the early days, starting with Anne Chauvin's being taken in at the beginning of winter 1839. Then, in connection with the General Chapter of 12 December

1847, he makes a vital observation on the history of the Congregation, 'From then on, it became the habit to date its origins from the rule and exercises of the "petit rocher" (see Chapter 5); a legend took shape side by side with history, not without altering it and reversing the roles.'

But being so close to the events—the Abbé Le Pailleur, who died on 20 December 1895, still enjoyed great esteem—and rather than collide head-on with accepted ideas, he avoided accusing the Abbé Le Pailleur in person, even though the legend was entirely to the latter's benefit. He was careful, indeed, to emphasise his good qualities as occasion demanded, leaving to others the job of turning the key which he had inserted in the lock.

This did not prevent him from being the first to insist on the role of Father Massot (he writes *Massat*) and the influence of the Brothers of St John of God, over which the circular letters of the Abbé Le Pailleur and those writings under his control maintain a studious silence.

The Abbé Leroy put all his personal papers relating to Jeanne Jugan into a cardboard box, and this box, alas, is no more. Here is the statement of the priest who felt obliged to carry out that irreparable act of destruction,

On my arrival at Bécherel in November 1931, I found a big cardboard packet, carefully sealed and bearing this note: *Confidential. To be destroyed unread.* I kept the package in the church safe until the death of Mademoiselle Leroy, who was the Abbé Leroy's sister. On her death-bed, Mlle Leroy confided to me that the package contained a certain number of important papers concerning Jeanne Jugan . . . several of the Abbé Le Pailleur's letters . . . official reports . . . letters from Rome . . . the package had been given her by her brother when he was dying, with instructions to burn the lot. Not having dared to take it on herself to carry out the last wishes of the deceased, she entrusted the responsibility for doing this to Canon Duplessix, the then parish priest and Dean of Bécherel. When I arrived, I found the documents in the church safe, but I had absolutely no idea where they came from or what they were about. At Mlle Leroy's request, in 1934, I destroyed all the documents thus deposited, without any inkling of their importance (Note by Canon Briend, former parish priest of Bécherel).

One year later, the preliminary inquiry with a view to Jeanne's beatification began.

ARSÈNE HELLEU (1882–1951)

In 1935, Canon Helleu was appointed Vice-Postulator by the Archbishop of Rennes, to conduct the diocesan inquiry with a view to Jeanne Jugan's beatification. He worked on this, very conscientiously, very methodically and with deep admiration for Jeanne, from 1935 to 1939. He himself interrogated, or had statements taken from, all surviving witnesses of Jeanne Jugan's life, as also from those persons in a position to report the memories of eye-witnesses.

For the use of the public, he condensed the results of his researches into a short book, of no literary pretention but very objective: *Une grande bretonne, Jeanne Jugan, fondatrice des Petites Sœurs des Pauvres.*

The only matter for regret is that the author did not include references to the documents and testimonies which he used.

Later research has made it possible to correct a few matters of detail in it, but it will always be one of the major sources for the life of Jeanne Jugan.

III   TEXT OF THE MEMORIAL ADDRESSED TO THE FRENCH ACADEMY TO SOLICIT THE AWARDING OF THE PRIX MONTYON TO JEANNE JUGAN

Commune of Saint-Servan
District of Saint-Malo
(Ille-et-Vilaine)

The undersigned, being witnesses to the heroic charity of a poor woman who for several years past has devoted herself to relieving the poor in the town of Saint-Servan (Ille-et-Vilaine), as will appear hereunder, believe it their duty to make such noble-hearted virtue known and to submit it to the Members of the Commission concerned with the awards for merit founded by M. de Montyon. Furthermore, the undersigned declare that the action which they now take has in no way been suggested to them by the person so recommended but that they, unprompted, informed the said poor woman of their intention in this matter. She, far from regarding herself as deserving of praise, pleaded with tears that her name should not be mentioned, but eventually gave her consent in the interests of her poor.

Jeanne Jugan was born of poor but honest and virtuous parents at Cancale, a small seaport, on 28 October 1792. Obliged to leave the paternal roof by reason of her family's poverty, she came to Saint-Servan at the age of twenty-five. Here she worked with great fidelity in a number of private houses, where her conduct was always one of perfect regularity. Among other persons with whom she took service was an unmarried elderly lady completely given over to good works, and there it was her chief delight to second her beloved mistress in the pious exercise of her charity. The latter having died, Jeanne went to live on her own, having no income and working for her living. Urged by a yearning to do good, however, she was not long in finding an opportunity for exercising her zeal.

Although it had a fair-sized population, and a population of seafarers who, all too often decimated by the perils of the sea, left their aged parents without support, Saint-Servan had no hospice or other place to admit the indigent aged of either sex. As a consequence, many unfortunate old people were exposed to every kind of hardship there. Their sorry state moved Jeanne's heart to compassion; she decided to come to their help. But how was she to go about it? She has no money—what of that? She puts her trust in God. Early in the winter of 1839, she learns that a poor, infirm and blind old woman has just lost her sister, the only person in the world who would look after her and beg her bread for her. Moved by her plight, Jeanne has her moved into her house and adopts her as her mother. Feeding this first arrival is no great worry to her: to support her, she will work longer into the night.[1]

Shortly afterwards comes a former maidservant, who has served her employers faithfully and without wages until their deaths, they having fallen on hard times. Not only serving them thus, she had also spent all her savings on them and then, having nothing left, had ended by begging for them and herself too. After their deaths, this woman, now weak and infirm, tells Jeanne of her sad plight. The latter at once and gladly takes her in.

This double conquest does but excite her zeal. No longer able to take in other unfortunates, her house being too small, she rents a larger one, moving into it on 1 October 1841. A month later, her new house is completely full; twelve poor old women find a refuge in it. But how is Jeanne to feed them? What little money she had saved is soon used up. Her charity then makes her resourceful. Since I have no more bread to give them, says she, all right, I shall go and beg for some; indeed I am better suited to the task than these poor things, broken down as they are by age and infirmity. And this is how she puts her idea into practice: she asks each of her poor people for the names of the benevolent persons accustomed to help them, then goes and solicits their alms herself. All readily consent and with good reason, for whereas in the past these unfortunates had the fatigue and humiliation of begging, and often misused what was given them, Jeanne now does the task for them, and each donor is sure that his alms will be put to good use.

Meanwhile, people start visiting Jeanne's poor house; public interest is aroused by such a good cause. The time has come, it is felt, to provide a refuge for the forsaken aged. Several charitable people collaborate to procure a house with more room in it. The house is acquired. It is made over to Jeanne, but no more can be done. So she is warned that, if the number of her poor people gets any larger, she will have to provide for their board and lodging herself. No matter; Jeanne agrees, believing that

---

[1] This first woman's name was Anne Chauvin, the widow Hannaux, who is still alive. The maid's name was Isabelle Queru; she died ten months ago in Jeanne's house.

Providence, having served her so well hitherto, will not default on her; and she joyfully enters her new home on 1 October 1842.

Soon, instead of twelve poor people, she has twenty; and after twenty, thirty; a year later, at the end of 1843, she has forty, and today—bless her!—the family around her numbers sixty-five poor wretches of both sexes, all of them old or infirm, or crippled, or limbless, or weak-minded, or suffering from incurable diseases, all snatched from the squalor of their garrets or from the shame of begging in the streets, and many snatched from the vices which vagrancy brings with it.

But who could do justice to this young woman's zeal in gathering in the poor! How often, herself going to seek them out in their dismal corners, she has persuaded them to go with her or, if they could not walk, has picked them up like a precious burden and cheerfully carried them off to her house! One day, she learns that an old man of seventy-two, Rodolphe Lainé, formerly a sailor, unpensioned, is living forsaken in a damp little cellar. She goes there, she sees a man with haggard face, covered in half-rotten rags, lying in what has once been straw but is now no more than a hideous dung-heap. This unfortunate had a stone for pillow; his cellar was underneath a house lived in by poor people who used to give him a few scraps of bread, and he had been living in this way for the previous two years. Moved by liveliest compassion at the sight, Jeanne went off, confided in a charitable acquaintance what she had just seen, and came back a moment later with a shirt and clean clothes. Having changed the old man's clothes, she takes this new guest back to her house, and today he enjoys good health. One might cite many other incidents of the same kind. She took in a little girl of five, a crippled orphan called Thérèse Poinso, whom no one wanted; on another occasion, a girl of fourteen, Jeanne Louette, whose unnatural parents had abandoned her on leaving our town; she took this unhappy girl in, as she was being dragged off to a place of prostitution. One day, a woman of loose morals, no longer meaning to support her old mother, the widow Colinet, brought her and threw her down in the street outside Jeanne's house; this poor woman had a horrible ulcer on her leg: reason for her to be received with even greater kindness. Another day, in mid-winter, in biting cold weather, at night-fall, two little children aged between nine and ten, from the depths of Lower Brittany, who had run away from home because there was nothing to eat there, were found wandering about our streets, knocking at every door. No one would take the poor little creatures in, because they had no money. The word rang out, 'Take them to Jeanne!' Jeanne did indeed take them in and feed them, until through the good offices of the Administration, whom she informed about them, they were returned to their parents' home. (Except for these two children, the other unfortunate people whom Jeanne has taken in, those named above and others, are domiciled in Saint-Servan.)

Stimulated by her example, three persons have joined her to share her cares and labours. These latter, with admirable devotedness and even to the detriment of their health, attend to all the heaviest jobs indoors, while outside Jeanne tirelessly subdivides herself into as many pieces as she has poor people to care for. She is forever on the go, whatever the weather, with a basket over her arm, and this she always brings home full. For not only, as we have already said, does she collect alms from the charitable people who wish to help her for the sake of the poor whom she has living in her house and who no longer besiege their doors, but with pious industry she also collects the remains from their tables, old linen and worn-out clothes; and thus, what would otherwise be wasted helps her to feed and clothe her poor people. In pleading their cause she is truly eloquent; she has often been known to burst into tears when explaining their needs. And so it is hard to refuse her, and she has nearly always succeeded in melting even the hardest of hearts. Even so, she is never importunate: if refused, she goes away at once, never showing the slightest sign of displeasure but saying, 'I'm sure you will help us another time.'

She has truly thrown in her lot with the poor; she dresses like them in what she is given; she lives on left-overs as they do, always making a point of keeping the best bits for those who are sick or more infirm; and the persons assisting her copy her example.

Lastly, order reigns in this house. The work is organised there.

A doctor of medicine is so kind as to give free consultations to those who are sick; he has even set up a little dispensary in it. The poor are treated kindly and kept very clean. This is common knowledge to everyone who has visited the house, and the old people there are happy to attest the same.

Thus, by great effort and by the simple means which she has thought fit to adopt and which cause inconvenience to no one, Jeanne Jugan has not only won the confidence of the town but has succeeded in snatching sixty-five old people from cold and want, has rid our streets of the hideous spectacle of their beggary and in less than four years has laid the foundations of a proper hospice or, as it is generally called, a home for the aged and infirm poor.

We have thought it our duty to describe to the Members responsible for allocating the awards for merit, some part of the good which this poor woman is doing, and if their favourable judgment sees fit to recognise such zeal and charity, we for our part are sure that the reward bestowed on her will contribute further to the welfare of her beloved poor.

Signed: M. J. Hay de Bonteville, Honorary Canon, parish priest of Saint-Servan; E. Girodroux; Le Maréchal; Dupont; De Bon; Jevin; H. Longueville; Louyer-Villermay; Moutardier; J. Turmel; Bourdin; P. Roger; Du Haut Cilly; Bourdase; E. Gouazon.

The Mayor of the Commune of Saint-Servan, while authenticating the fifteen signatures of the members of the Municipal Council and that of the parish priest, placed hereabove, certifies that the facts mentioned in the account are personally known to him.

Saint-Servan, 21 December 1844
Signed: Douville

The undersigned member of the General Council, acting as Sub-Prefect of the District of Saint-Malo, by delegation of the Prefect of Ille-et-Vilaine, the holder of that office being on holiday, has had all the good works of Miss Jeanne Jugan brought to his attention. The testimony of the honourable persons whom he has heard has been unanimous concerning all the facts recorded in the report hereto appended. He therefore most earnestly recommends this virtuous woman to the kindly interest of the members of the Commission set up to distribute the awards for merit founded by M. de Montyon.

The Councillor General
Signed: Louis Blaire

IV NOTES ON THE SCENES FROM HOSPITALLER LIFE IN LONDON, PAINTED DURING JEANNE JUGAN'S LIFETIME, BY JAMES COLLINSON (1825–81)

James Collinson, a student of the Royal Academy, joined his fellow-students Holman Hunt and Dante Gabriel Rossetti in the Pre-Raphaelite Brotherhood, an association of seven artists, of whom five were painters; he withdrew from the group after becoming a Catholic.

First picture (between pages 86 and 87)

Known for his attention to detail and for his mastery in presenting it, Collinson has carried verisimilitude to the point of writing the name and address of the old blind woman, Mary Hayes, on the envelope lying on the floor. Admitted on 15 January 1868 to the Little Sisters' house in Portobello Road, London, Mary Hayes died there on 9 October 1869.

Author's note. The text of the original manuscript has been retained unemended: it gives 28 October instead of 25 October for Jeanne Jugan's date of birth; a few proper names are wrongly spelt; Rodolphe Laisné was 76 years old, not 72.

The scene is remarkable for its trueness to life and for its exactness of observation. The aged people are vividly portrayed; the Little Sisters, all of them young—the Congregation had not been thirty years in existence—seem as though steeped in the advice given them by Jeanne Jugan, 'Little ones, take good care of the aged, for in them you are caring for Jesus himself.' 'If you are with the aged, be kind, very kind.' 'When you are with the poor, give yourself with all your heart.'

Rediscovered by chance in England in 1973, this picture is now at the Congregation's mother-house.

Second picture (between pages 182 and 183)

In a letter of 15 June 1875, Fr Lelièvre, an auxiliary priest of the Congregation, speaks to his friend Louis Marest about this picture, painted in the Little Sisters' house in London,

> Look for a man standing up, who is handing out the bread . . . This man is Richard. [Richard Bentley, who had just died after fourteen years spent with the Little Sisters.]
>
> From the moment that there was an infirmary and sick people in the house . . . he asked for and was given the post of assistant to the Sister Infirmarian, a position which he filled, until the month of May last, with all the exactitude, all the zeal, all the patience, that the most devoted of Sisters might have brought to it. He slept among his sick people, was at their service night and day, never showed other than a cheerful, contented face . . . I do not think, for all the time I knew him, that he lost for so much as a quarter of an hour his sense of the presence of God . . . O Richard, if there is a soul on earth of whom I feel envious and of whom I am still a little bit jealous even now, it is you! In whom have I seen, as in him, such faith and hope united in such charity? His face and expression said all; his life too says all. I forgot to mention that when he entered the house, he was as deaf as a post. He bore this infirmity with the same equanimity as all the rest. They say that his last moments were those of a saint, and I believe it! Now, all I can say is this, 'Richard, remember that I was your friend and that, although I knew you when you were very poor, I never treated you otherwise than with respect!'

All trace of this picture has been lost, but a photograph of it taken by the painter himself still survives.